School Eth

David O'Malley SDB

David O'Malley
provides internet support at
www.salesians.org.uk/chap/

Don Bosco

Artwork by Val O'Brien

Credits

Used by permission
Renewing the Vision: A Framework for Catholic Youth Ministry
(United States Conference of Catholic Bishops Washington 1997)
Sr Barbara Brent, School Chaplaincy - Some Reflections in The Pastoral Review
(Jan/Feb 2005)

We have made every effort to contact copyright holders and seek their permission to use their material. If any infringement of copyright has occurred, we offer our apologies and will correct any errors in future editions.

Dedication

Miss **Rosie Woods**. Carmel College, St Helens, whose encouragement and expertise have been vital in developing this resource.
Thanks also to the following for their support and encouragement

Rev Dr Jan Cheeseman
Chaplain Harrogate Ladies College

Canon Brendan Clover
The Woodard Schools

Maggie Cascioli
Chair of the Association of Chaplains in Catholic Education

Ros Stuart Buttle
Director of Ushaw College online training school

Fr J A Quigley
Diocesan Department of Education, Birmingham

Bernard Stuart
Chaplaincy Co-ordinator for Salford Diocese

Michael Georgiou
Chair of The Salesian Chaplaincy Group

Don Bosco Publications © 2008
Thornleigh House
Bolton BL1 6PQ
Tel 01204 308 811
www.don-bosco-publications.co.uk
Printed by Printoff Graphic Arts Ltd

The worthwhile survival of our Catholic Schools
depends on the continually renewed promotion of their Gospel-inspired ethos.

In these pages,
Chaplains and would-be chaplains will find an affirmation of their contribution,
a challenge to appreciate its scope,
and much practical wisdom, hewn from experience, for implementation.

Central to the author's purpose
is the need for chaplaincy to be dynamically owned by senior management.
They alone can create the atmosphere in which it can flourish.
All concerned with Catholic schooling will benefit from this vision.

Read on!

+ Brian M. Noble, Bishop of Shrewsbury

Contents

Foreword

A school is not a parish, but needs to work closely with the parish in which it is located. School and parish together have a complementary task. A parish is not a school; it is particularly charged with communicating the faith and inviting people to accept the message of Christ. Therefore the church door is open for everyone, inviting them to come in and look, and decide freely to remain or not. A school instead is presenting the mystery of our complex relationship with God, offering information about the basic craving of everyone to get in touch with the mystery which is present in the depth of everyone's existence. The task of a chaplain, in a school therefore, is to make sure that the climate there is such that the mystery can be spoken about and experienced.

The greatest task of school leadership is to assure a positive climate and atmosphere in the school. The chaplain's first target group, therefore, is the leadership of the school and its members of staff. In the first place, the chaplain will help to build up a group of people, teachers, and students alike, who form the pastoral heart of the school and create a Gospel climate. More than simply preparing celebrations, which are evidently important, it is necessary that the chaplain create a mentality that these events form part of a whole-school unity and that these events have a strong impact on the whole school. As regards relationships with the students, the chaplain is called to be close to them in a friendly and healthy way. One thing the chaplain must avoid is a limited focus on either the neediest or the most gifted or the most troublesome students. A chaplain should have other functions in the school, and not be labelled simply as a member of the religious education team, since religion is much more than an academic matter, but rather a lived experience. To this end, the leadership group of the school has an important part to play in supporting the chaplain's role and creating the climate for living the gospel and connecting that experience to the home and the parish. The relationships in school carry the values, the witness and the experience of being loved in a healthy life-giving way. That is why Saint John Bosco described religious education as being largely a matter of the heart and the chaplain is there to help that climate of Gospel love to flourish.

+ Luc Van Looy SDB
Bishop of Gent
(Ecclesiastical Assistant of World Union of Catholic Teachers)

Introduction

Making a decision on the title of this book has been difficult. In the beginning we saw this publication as a handbook for chaplains in school: a useful structure within which chaplains could work. As it was shared with a wider group of chaplains it became obvious that the information in the book was equally relevant to the decision makers in school. Later still, the close links between chaplaincy and the promotion of a Christian ethos were seen as the wider context within which all chaplaincies needed to be viewed.

Chaplaincy is an ancient ministry and an emerging profession in many communities and institutions today. Prisons, hospitals, universities and military chaplaincies are all in a process of rapid development of the chaplaincy role. School chaplaincy too is in the process of changing from a clerical to a largely lay ministry, at a time of tension between a secular and a faith-based approach to learning. This time of change creates an opportunity to rethink and focus chaplaincy so that it can penetrate the veneer of secular thinking and reach down into the richer roots of the Christian tradition in new ways.

Chaplaincy is one of the most flexible and ecumenical roles in a school setting, one that can support and energise the distinctive nature of Christian education. The person of the chaplain is a living sign of a school's commitment to ethos, a sign that the Catholic Bishops of England and Wales have urged every secondary school to embrace. This book is an attempt to outline the range of possibilities involved in chaplaincy, the skills needed for the role and some professional approaches that can support a school as it develops a broad-based chaplaincy.

Chaplaincy provision is not identical with a chaplain. The content of this book cannot be used as check list for an individual chaplain because no individual chaplain could fulfil all of the demands outlined in this book. The material in the book should be seen as an ideal map of chaplaincy within which a chaplain, guided and supported by leadership, can make a sustained impact. The specific tasks of a chaplain need to be identified through a negotiation between the dominant needs of the school and the particular gifts of the chaplain. Chaplaincy provision, as a whole, remains the remit of the leadership of the school. The leadership team needs to create the setting within which a chaplain can be effective and establish clear priorities, whilst maintaining significant flexibility in the chaplain's role.

This book is aimed at those who need to understand, create and manage the chaplaincy as a professional role within a school. How far that professionalism is established will depend upon the recognition by other colleagues in school and the willingness of leadership to take budgeted risks in employing full-time lay chaplains in the years ahead. The experience of chaplaincy suggests that it works best as a second career, building upon a professionalism and skills learned elsewhere. Such individuals come to chaplaincy with a clear understanding of good practice, line-management and the kind of boundaries associated with any profession. Such candidates, showing a pastoral approach and ability to reflect theologically, integrate more easily into the rhythms of work in school and are prepared to establish pastoral relationships with the staff.

Much of the content in this book focuses on the need for clarity about the chaplaincy role and the structures a school might need to adopt to integrate chaplaincy into the patterns of planning in school life. There is however a part of chaplaincy that will not fit the normal pattern of timetabled colleagues. Chaplains have a contemplative as well as an active dimension to their role. They are contemplatives in action. Therefore chaplains need some time to reflect theologically on what is happening in the school. They need to be the still point in the whirlwind of school life. This dimension of the role needs to be reflected in the planning and evaluation of the work of a chaplain and above all else understood and encouraged by those who provide the chaplain with line-management. The presence of someone who is reflecting theologically in a school setting can be enlightening, comforting but, at times, disturbingly prophetic. Unfortunately it is the part of the role that can easily be lost if there is no adequate support. In that case the chaplain is drawn into the whirlwind too much and, like some missionaries abroad they risk *going native* and blending in with values which they should in fact challenge.

Above all else a school chaplain must take the personal risk of becoming a symbol and an instrument of Christ as a bringer of life, of meaning and of healing. The idealism attached to the role can put the chaplain under pressures that other colleagues do not carry. The chaplain has to be seen as constantly approachable, encouraging, forgiving and able to hold many secrets appropriately. This can place further burdens upon the person of the chaplain and makes the provision of regular line-management and non-managerial supervision essential for the healthy fulfilment of this role. The employment of a lay chaplain therefore demands a different process of recruitment and support than that of other school roles. The presence of a chaplain also requires the school to establish a chaplaincy plan which can orientate the chaplain's work and not leave them adrift in the school.

Each appointment of a new chaplain will see a little more development and appreciation of this emerging profession in education. Each chaplain can be legitimately challenged to become more accountable by the school so that the chaplain's work can be integrated into the whole-school planning process. Each school needs to explore ways of working with chaplains and help to share good practice through the emerging diocesan network of chaplains.

Chaplaincy is a practical and innovative way to extend the tradition of the Church into contemporary culture. Chaplains can discover the treasure of meaning buried in the ordinary patterns of a school community and unlock the energy and vocational commitment of staff and pupils that they may go that extra mile in the service of others. For many people in school the chaplain may become the only friendly face of the Church that can open hearts and bring hope to many. Together with the headteacher, the chaplain is a spiritual leader in the school and the missionary the Church needs in a secular society. The schools that commit to employing them, supporting them and developing their role in school, will be blessed a hundredfold for their endeavours.

The Ancient Story of Chaplaincy

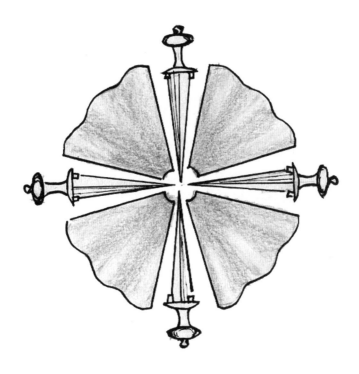

The story of chaplaincy begins at the gate to the city of Amiens in 337 CE. Martin, a young soldier in the Roman army, was walking into the city during a bitterly cold winter. The crowds were hurrying past a half-naked beggar who was close to death. Martin, unpaid and having only his military uniform, stopped and looked at the man who gazed back at him expectantly, with hand outstretched. After a slight hesitation, Martin took out his sword and then removed his cloak and sliced it through the middle giving one half to the man and using the other half to cover himself again.

Some bystanders laughed at him and the ridiculous way he looked, wearing only half a cloak. But other bystanders felt ashamed that this poor soldier, from his poverty, had helped the beggar and made a difference, whilst they with money in their pockets, had ignored the beggar completely, walking away when challenged by Martin's actions.

Later that night Martin had a dream, he saw a vision of Christ himself wearing the half cloak and saying to others *Look at the cloak that Martin gave me today, and he only a poor soldier and a layman too.* The dream so affected Martin that he tried to leave the army and in 339 CE he was released into civilian life. From there he went on to work for the poor and increase awareness of the presence of God in ordinary people. He created a number of communities and became a Church leader. He died at Tours in 397 CE.

His cloak, or half a cloak, became a precious object in military and royal circles. It became a spiritual symbol for the whole community. The cloak was used in the taking of oaths and was carried into battle and came to symbolise all that was best in humanity, a symbol of the spiritual dignity of each person and a powerful reminder of the need to seek God in ordinary things. The cloak was called a *capella* - a cape. It was kept in a tent or in a building that came to be called a *cappella* or chapel. The person assigned to look after this sacred relic was called the *capellano* or chaplain. The chaplain would control access to the sacred symbol and organise prayers and ceremonies for the community to celebrate the spirituality it signified. These were the first people to be called chaplains. They began firstly in the army, then in royal courts, later in hospitals and more recently in education.

The story highlights some key features of chaplaincy:

- It was inspired by a lay person's act of listening and serving the needy.

- It is based around the God-given dignity of each person in the community.

- It is a form of service that challenges others to think about their own lives.

- It involves safeguarding and celebrating the spiritual treasures of a community.

- It is a ministry rooted in prayer and reflection on Jesus and the Gospels.

St Martin of Tours' symbolic act casts a long shadow across Church history, reaching the second Vatican Council and our own multi-cultural world. It touches all forms of chaplaincy in health, military and educational settings and points to the unique combination of religion, reflection and service all focused on a specific group's needs at a particular time and place.

These five dimensions represent an insight into chaplaincy that is rooted in the tradition and experience of the Christian community. Before moving on to more recognisable and current descriptions of the role it is helpful to explore the more intuitive approach that this story opens up.

1 Listening and serving

Martin shared the same experience as other people on the road into Amiens that winter. He acted differently because he heard the cry of the poor man and took the time to stop. He engaged with a personal need and responded as best he could from his own resources. The story reminds us that chaplains have to stop and listen. That means listening to pupils and staff who are left out in the cold, *wasting time* with people on corridors and in staff rooms and recognising needs even when unspoken. The story reminds us that chaplains need to put their personal gifts at the service of the most needy in the community in which they are called to work.

2 Recognising an individual's dignity

The story tells us that the beggar at the gate was Christ himself and that whatever we do for the least of our brothers and sisters we do for Jesus. This rather pious observation takes the ordinary pastoral care for people into an almost mystical encounter with God especially in the struggling members of a school community. The chaplain's role is to keep reminding the school community that the trouble-maker, the time-watching teacher and the truant are all children of God. How we treat them will be the litmus test of whether we are living the Gospel as a school community.

3   A form of service that challenges

Martin took action in public in a way that divided opinion. From one act he gained both ridicule and respect and above all he made people think. This conscious action in public is a major strategy in chaplaincy in school. To influence a large community it is not enough to appear only in church or prayer settings. A chaplain has to design actions that will animate the whole community towards justice and peace. Those actions may be aimed specifically at certain groups but their impact should be school wide. A chaplain who is always passive and waits for others to come to them is missing this prophetic dimension to the role.

4   Safeguarding & celebrating spiritual treasures

The chaplain's task was originally to guard and celebrate the sacred symbols of the court, of the army or of the community. In school chaplaincy, the role is exactly the same; ensuring that the Gospels, the sacraments and the traditions of the Christian community are respected, reverenced and absorbed into practice is part of this ministry. At one level this means ensuring that prayer, liturgy and sacraments are well prepared, that symbols of faith are displayed and given due honour. It also means building bridges between those of different faith and no faith so that these treasures can be embraced as far as possible by the whole community of the school.

5   Rooted in prayer and reflection on Jesus and the Gospel

Martin walked through the gate at Amiens and heard God speak in a beggar. He could not have heard if he had not been listening and immersed in the presence of God himself. The chaplain, in order to fulfil the role must also be prayer-centred and have part of their life and timetable focused on stillness and scripture. There is a spiritual asceticism about the chaplain's role that will always elude job descriptions. It will be the chaplain's task to live a prayerful and disciplined spiritual life. The effects of that inner work will emerge in holiness and wisdom certainly but also in a prophetic zeal that may, at times, disturb the assumptions of others in the school community.

This brief reflection will be returned to later in the text as a structure to help schools evaluate their chaplaincy provision. One of the main tasks of this book is to provide a background to the tradition of chaplaincy and also to suggest the professional and pastoral guidelines within which this tradition needs to operate today. More structure will be needed for chaplaincy as it becomes a more established strategy in the development of faith schools and the *Every Child Matters* agenda in England and Wales.[1] Educators need to know how chaplaincy works, what its priorities are and how such a service integrates with other school systems. This book is an attempt by a practising chaplain to address the way that chaplaincy can be developed alongside the current professional demands of education.

In secular cultures the need for chaplaincy in schools is likely to grow since it can offer the flexibility and the invitational approach to the Gospel that other aspects of school find difficult to provide. Governors and school leadership will find in chaplaincy a way to recognise and develop the spiritual dimension of the faith school. Chaplaincy becomes another effective tool that can support and extend the school's own spiritual agenda, without compromising on the more target-led approaches to education which are in vogue at present. This short book is offered to all the policy makers in schools to inform them about the strengths of chaplaincy, to outline its strong tradition and to offer some structures for starting, managing and evaluating chaplains in the complex educational environment of secondary education in a secular culture.

---

[1] http://www.everychildmatters.gov.uk/

Chapter One
The Nature of School Chaplaincy

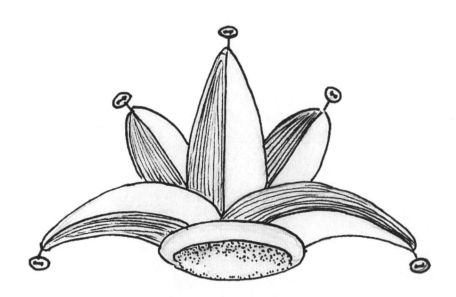

Chaplains have been involved in education for hundreds of years providing a listening ear and as organisers of the spiritual dimension of the school community. Many of those roles have been filled by ordained clergy who brought their pastoral and liturgical skills into school settings. In many schools where a named chaplain has been unavailable, other staff have shared aspects of the chaplain's role, especially in pastoral areas where spiritual support and prayer have been needed.

As education has expanded and the pace of educational change has accelerated, the need for chaplaincy has increased and it is ever more difficult for the chaplaincy provision to be made through non-specialist staff. Indeed it is becoming increasingly difficult to recruit committed Catholic staff for any role in the school. This places increased importance on recruiting committed and qualified Christians. The provision of chaplaincy, in a fast-paced secondary school, involves a high level of skills and also clarity of thought that demands some specific training and management. The following thoughts highlight just some of the aspects of the chaplain's role within a school, serving as a background to the more specific issues explored later in this chapter. The contrast between these descriptions of a chaplain and those of a classroom teacher, for example, should remind the school leadership of the unique importance of this role and also the isolation that can sometimes be felt by chaplains and the support that might be needed if they are to succeed in their role.

Chaplain as minister

The chaplain in a school is a minister of the Church. The chaplain may or may not be ordained but is always a minister of the Christian faith called to offer a public proclamation of the Gospel within the school community. In school they represent both Gospel values in action and also the institution of the Church. This dual aspect of ministry takes a chaplain into a way of working that has four dimensions:

- Engaging with common concerns so that the chaplain can be seen to be serving Christ in others.

- Looking at the whole-school situation and identifying where good may grow and seeking the removal of whatever stands in the way of progress.

- Making sense of what is happening in school and in the lives of individuals through the Christian story, the sacraments, worship and the discernment that happens in prayer.

- Creating projects and encouraging relationships that lead toward a change of mind and heart through activities that have silence and contemplation built into them for the good of all.[2]

The work of the chaplain spirals through these aspects of Christian ministry and makes many hidden demands upon the chaplain's own learning, spirit and energy. Therefore, the chaplain is not primarily a pastoral worker in the school, nor a formal teacher in the classroom. Instead the chaplain represents and uncovers the presence of Christ in the school community, in a specific and focused role.

Chaplain as educator

The chaplain is not usually involved in formal education but adopts a role that involves non-formal education within a formal school structure. The main teaching aids used by a chaplain are, personal example, conversation, liturgy and project work at various levels in the school community. Much of the education achieved by the chaplain happens on corridors rather than classrooms, it is sometimes unplanned and its outcomes are often uncertain. There is no textbook and the only curriculum is that which is provided within the conversation that emerges with individuals and with groups.

For these reasons, sometimes school leaders do not recognise the chaplain as an educator. At a time when education has become tied to assessment, measured outcomes and tighter curriculum control the non-formal style of education can be undervalued. One of the largest differences between the classroom educator and the chaplain is that education happens through the free choice of the pupil or staff member who engages with the chaplain. The learning contract is always personal and voluntary. The timing of that educational encounter is also in the hands of the learner who approaches the chaplain. Yet, despite all these contrasts, what the chaplain does during the day is educational in a way that can touch hearts, reduce alienation and awaken gifts and dreams that can lead to Gospel living and fullness of life.

Sometimes, through liturgy and in some styles of project work, the chaplain can appear to have a more formal teaching role but in general the informal role tends to dominate. In a similar way, most good classroom teachers can move into a non-formal mode of teaching and learning when they respond to non-curriculum demands in young people and enter into voluntary activity on their behalf. The

---

[2] See Ann Loader, Ministry in The New SCM Dictionary of Christian Spirituality, (London SCM 2005).

value of such non-formal encounters lies in the process that develops with individuals and groups rather than any specific measured outcomes. Much of the learning is spontaneous, unplanned and not easy to catch, despite a certainty that learning has happened. More theory and structure about the non-formal education approach can be found at the website for informal education hosted by George Williams College, London.[3]

The implication of this dimension of chaplaincy is that the role demands a high level of knowledge and skills which have to be practised in a very demanding environment. The chaplain's role demands professionalism in education and a status that puts the chaplain on an equal standing with their classroom-based colleagues. Chaplains will be asked to work with small groups that will form and dissolve within a few weeks and achieve spiritual and personal growth in the majority of the group. They will be expected to engage with individual needs and group them where possible into therapeutic networks that lead to life and growth. They will be expected to analyse school situations with groups of staff and pupils in the light of the Gospel. The lay chaplain will only develop with a viable role if the quality of the work they can do is recognised and funded appropriately into the future. Otherwise the role will be only partially filled by young respondents who will need to leave the role in order to raise a family or by older applicants who can afford to take a substantial pay reduction. As with many aspects of Church life, the commitment to this role in school will be judged by the account book as much as by the book of the Gospel.

Sacramental chaplain

The word sacramental takes in more than the liturgical sacraments of the Church and has a meaning that extends even beyond any single religion. In its simplest form a sacrament is an outward sign of an inner spiritual reality. The bread, consecrated at a Eucharist, becomes an experience of the presence of the risen Christ. The water used in Baptism becomes a sign of a vital inner life and spirit in the baptised person. Sacraments reveal how human beings are in relationship with God and in this broad sense all of creation is a sacrament. Each event and every experience is an expression of God's presence echoed in wonder, curiosity, gratitude and awe within the human heart. Not that God is contained by creation, but rather all creation, life and especially human life, point beyond themselves towards God.

[3] http://www.infed.org/

The chaplain, working in school, is called to recognise and reverence the signs of God's presence in the school community. As well as preparing the liturgical celebration of the sacraments, the chaplain needs to celebrate the daily sacraments of human love and life offered up each day in classroom and corridor. Seeing the presence of God in a pupil who shares their dinner money or recognising the prodigal son welcomed back into class by a teacher whom he has let down are part of the task of a chaplain. These are sacramental moments for one who has eyes to see them. In reality each relationship and every exchange during the school day is a potential encounter with the mystery of God. Part of the chaplain's role is to open the eyes of the whole school community to this depth and mystery, hidden within these ordinary moments and invite people into a relationship with the mystery of God in life.

The chaplain is also a sacrament in the way their role is lived out in school. Chaplains are spiritual figures in the school whose very presence provokes questions about life and its meaning. Chaplains live their faith visibly, making themselves available as an example for others to follow. They act and relate to others consciously as people who try to model the Gospel in their work. Similarly, a school that chooses a full-time chaplain is making a statement about the value it is placing on the inner and hidden life of the members of the school community. The chaplain becomes the outward sign of an inner and spiritual world that the school chooses to celebrate and develop. The chaplain, as a sacramental presence, reveals the sacred in every member of the school community and challenges them to hear the call and embrace the transforming energy that inner presence can offer to each person.

In promoting specific worship and sacramental liturgy, the chaplain is simply sharpening the focus of the lived experience of God's presence through the ordinary day. The school Eucharist therefore should reveal the real presence not simply in the bread and wine that is offered but also in the experience of the pupils and staff. The Sacrament of the Eucharist will then contain the meaning of each person and each event in the life of the school and give them deeper significance. The celebration of the sacraments at every level provides a pattern of meaning and a common language that can accompany every pupil into the future. These experiences will live in the memory of each pupil and call them back to the support of the Church that will be present in their lives wherever they may go and for as long as they are alive. The chaplain invites all people in the school community to a discipleship based on an inner call often aroused by outward signs. The chaplain works sacramentally.

Relationship with the whole school

Secondary schools today are highly complex. They remind me of a motor cycle display team I worked with in London. The precision timing of manoeuvres, the way that bikes crossed at various levels, jumped over gaps and went through hoops of fire took one's breath away. In a similar way, schools have processes that work at different levels with tight time limits, so that assessments and exams can be coordinated and pupils can go through the sometimes fiery hoops of reports and Parents' Evenings. Anyone wandering ignorantly through this complexity of planning and coordinated service of young people could wreak havoc. A chaplain, working at whole-school level, is called to work within these rhythms as part of an adult team. The projects and initiatives of the chaplaincy need to be coordinated within the primary task of formal education. Therefore a chaplain has to establish a relationship with a school that takes into account the changing patterns of working, the amount of free time, the tiredness of the staff and the pressures on examination groups.

The chaplain will be one member of staff among many who will be demanding extra commitment from young people and from staff. In my present role the school musical has now been placed in Advent and it would be unfair to propose any large school event in the weeks around that musical. On the other hand, the preparation of a musical provides a wonderful opportunity for an all-age school event that binds the community together into a celebration of God-given talent and trust. Good line-management is the key to a chaplain's whole-school relationship. Negotiating spaces for specific events, finding curriculum spaces within which to work, building Christian leadership programmes and so on need detailed planning and wide evaluation. Chaplaincy does not exist in a bubble in a school life. It has to be integrated alongside the ordinary life of the school.

There is another aspect of a chaplain's relationship to the whole school that is seldom mentioned. Listening is at the heart of the chaplain's role and every chaplain will need to develop the skill of being still and letting people talk honestly and safely. All too often, what people say to the chaplain will be sensitive and the chaplain might be the only recipient of such inner struggles. When such dark thoughts are isolated events they will tend to be personal issues, but when they emerge from a range of people the chaplain may be listening to the shadow side of the school life. Every school has a shadow side where the hidden hurts of the past emerge into resistance and conspiracy theories. Sometimes these shadows reveal a hidden truth that needs to be voiced but for the most part they need to be absorbed and earthed to safety by the chaplain. That process involves hearing the issues clearly, encouraging their communication to decision makers and placing such struggles in a wider vocational context for those involved.

The chaplain has a whole-school role and needs to be taken into the confidence of leadership and governing groups in order to fulfil the chaplaincy role. In broad terms, a chaplain needs to be informed and consulted. In return the chaplain needs to maintain confidentiality and offer regular feedback on whole-school issues. For many schools the chaplain will become the main conduit of information about parish links and also ecumenical and interfaith initiatives in the neighbourhood. There needs to be some space for these out of school contacts to be shared at whole-school level.

The relationship between the school and the chaplain is complex and in each case it will develop into a unique pattern. In order to capture some of the variety, a few images are offered below. None of them can say everything but together they may fill in some of the ways in which chaplaincy might be viewed in its relationship to the whole school.

Some chaplaincy images

Jester
In the court of the king, the Jester, like the chaplain, had a roving brief and was able to access all areas of the court. He was also able to speak the truth and challenge the king. At times, the chaplain who will have access to all areas of the school may see and have to share appropriately, things that may not be welcome to the whole school.

Parish Priest
The relationship between a priest and his parish can be seen as a model for the chaplain since it implies provision of pastoral and spiritual services for the school community, including the sacraments and a lived witness to the Gospel. The analogy breaks down in the area of authority which is very different in a school where the chaplain supports the spiritual leadership of the headteacher as the spiritual leader of the community.

Defragmenter
Those familiar with computers will recognise the role of defragmentation programs which re-organise files and create extra space on the computer. A

chaplain can be seen as one who helps people to link together their scattered experiences and pattern them into the shape of the Gospel, leaving room for further growth and development for the whole school as well as for individuals.

Still Point

In the whirlwind of school activity some schools need the chaplain to be a still point, *the eye of the storm* in school activity. The chaplain who has no classroom timetable and who plans well will always be able to stop and listen, walk with someone to their class and create pools of peace for others. Standing still in the storm can give the chaplain a unique whole-school insight that can be invaluable to the school community and those who make plans within it.

Ship's Navigator

When pupils were asked for an image of the school, the image of the ship at sea was very popular. The chaplain was seen as a navigator, warning of storms, recognising when the ship was straying off course and advising the captain. In a similar way, the pupils saw the chaplain as having a weather eye on school values and advising the headteacher.

Weaver

A weaver's skill lies in drawing threads into a pattern and using what is available to form a design that will make sense to others. In a similar way, the chaplain picks up the experience of the school and by reflection and conversation weaves them into a Gospel pattern. This can free up the goodwill, to make the experience of the school community more life-giving.

Prophet

The scriptures are full of images of individuals who challenged the community to be faithful to the word of God. Even in Christian schools, there may be policies and practices that compromise the Gospel. Chaplains, gifted by their schools with time for reflection, have a different perspective from which they can read the signs of the times earlier and perhaps more accurately than busier members of the school community. The chaplain has the task of reminding the school of Gospel values from within the community and encouraging faithfulness to that Gospel in every aspect of life.

These images and many more, illustrate the variety and subtlety of chaplaincy as a whole-school endeavour. They describe the task as the service of a whole-school community and not simply to the young people as a youth minister. The images suggest a role that is involved and yet a step back from total immersion so that there is time for reflection and prayer at the heart of the school. Three specific scriptural images underline the heart of chaplaincy for Christians: The Good Shepherd from John's Gospel[4], The Mustard Seed from Matthew's Gospel[5] and the Emmaus story from Luke's Gospel.[6] Each will be considered briefly below.

Good Shepherd

In the Gospel of John, Jesus compares himself to a good shepherd. Using images that would have been familiar to all his listeners, he describes the skill of the good shepherd and the shepherd's relationship with the sheep.

Such images, rooted in a rural landscape, take on a new significance when viewed in the context of leadership in schools and youth groups today. There are no wolves stalking school corridors and no lack of water and food for young people. However, pessimism, bullying and sadness roam many corridors and even set up home in the hearts of young people and colleagues. The aching in hearts is less likely to be a hunger for bread and more likely to be a hunger for recognition and reassurance. Awareness of these individual needs and the ability to protect, guide and lead people to life are the qualities of a good shepherd. In using these gifts, chaplains will find themselves entering the mind of Jesus, as they work professionally and genuinely with the young.

The chaplain needs to get to know people in the school individually and to notice how they manage the landscape of the school year. There are seasons in a school where patience wears thin, where the wolves of pessimism and frustration stalk the corridors, to emerge in bullying, shouting and over-reactions to genuine mistakes. A chaplain, walking the school, needs to know how to ease these tensions and protect the vulnerable. In a whole-school setting, the chaplain needs to identify these same wolves on the agendas of meetings and in the closed huddles of cliques in playgrounds and staff rooms.

The ability of the chaplain to create safe places for the vulnerable within the school day is a shepherding role worked out within the pastoral system in the school and with staff-support groups. Safety is ensured by the chaplain being available to all and yet belonging to no single group. A chaplain does not belong to a department, to the leadership team, or to the governing body. The chaplain listens in confidence and is prepared to speak unwelcome truths when

---

[4] Jn 10:1-18
[5] Mt 13:31-32
[6] Lk 24:13-35

necessary, laying aside the usual gentle approach, at times, to challenge what may be harming members of the school community.

Finally, the chaplain, like the good shepherd has no fixed pasture. Chaplaincy has no curriculum but takes its curriculum from the changing needs of the community as they are presented. Therefore pet projects, clever schemes and regular provision all have to give way to the changing needs of young people and staff. When chaplaincy has not changed its shape for a number of years it could be that it has begun to serve the needs of adults rather than those of the young people. This major theme in chaplaincy will be revisited later, in the context of the chaplain as a youth minister.

Mustard Seed

The image of the mustard seed is appropriate to all educators who plant seeds in the lives of young people in the hope that some of them will grow to fullness of life. For the chaplain, this image is central to the process of ministry because, unlike other aspects of education much of the work of chaplains is small and hidden. Small gestures, such as the quiet word in the ear, the card to a member of staff on the anniversary of a wedding or a bereavement, being present in a playground on rainy days or dropping into classes where staff may be struggling. All these actions are hidden away in the life of the school. Encouraging words, compassion and praise are scattered like seeds through the school during a chaplaincy day. Small projects too, planted in hope may look small within the wider movement of school plans; yet, if these projects are planned with kindness, if they arise from the Gospel and lead to growth they can become much more. The quiet acts and small projects of a chaplain can grow into a huge network of loving kindness in a school and create many opportunities for the weary and hungry *to come and rest in its branches.*[7] Chaplains are people who need to have time for the little things and recognise the way that God often chooses what is weak and insignificant to surprise the wise and the clever.[8]

Emmaus

The third scriptural image for chaplaincy comes from the end of the Gospel of Luke where an encounter with the risen Jesus is experienced. The two disciples going home to Emmaus after the crucifixion were depressed and disillusioned by the cruel end that Jesus had met. When the risen Jesus joined their conversation they did not recognise him but told him their sad story. Jesus listened and felt the

---

[7] Mt 13:32
[8] For the scriptural reference to this comment refer to I Cor 1:27.

heaviness of their hearts. Then he began to trace deeper patterns of meaning through those same events and helped the two disciples to see things differently. Their hearts began to burn within them as he talked and they invited him to stay with them. In the evening the two disciples recognised Jesus in the way he broke the bread at the meal. At that point he disappeared from them and the two disciples left immediately to tell the good news in Jerusalem.

Chaplains often see this story as a model for their informal work with young people and staff. The story emphasises the importance of getting alongside people and walking at their pace. It reminds chaplains that their first duty is to listen, not only with the ears but with the heart, to what people say. The Emmaus story is a reminder too that we meet Jesus in each other and in the ordinary events of life. Knowing the scripture and tradition of the Church is a vital aspect of the work of the chaplain which is highlighted by this story. A chaplain who *walks* the school will see many parables in action. Chaplains will see self-sacrificing love and the goodness of God in every playground if they become familiar with the emotional patterns that underlie the scriptures and the wisdom upon which the Christian tradition is built.

The Emmaus story is a reminder that every chaplain needs to engage in heartfelt conversations. The chaplain's role cannot be simply mechanical: it is always personal. The pastoral relationship is the sacred space where heart speaks to heart and in that holy exchange Christ is a quiet presence. The chaplain is called to recognise that quiet presence and let it grow towards a sharper focus. Conversation then becomes a form of evangelisation; a proclamation of the Gospel in every heartfelt exchange.

The turning point in the Emmaus story happens in the context of a meal where bread is broken. This aspect of the story reminds the chaplain that all their work leads towards the breaking of the bread of life in the school community. At times, this will be a hidden aspect of school life but the chaplain needs to link the hidden sacrifices, which people in school constantly make, with the sacraments and traditions of a Eucharistic community. The Eucharist does not just mean the Mass. It means breaking open the experience of life, forgiveness, sharing the word, recognising our dignity as God's children and being sent to one another in service. These aspects of Eucharist are lived every day in every life but reach their sharpest focus and impact in the sacramental celebration of the Eucharist to which the entire chaplain's work should point.

Finally the Emmaus story highlights the circular pattern of a chaplain's work. The two disciples ended up back where they started, in Jerusalem, where the risk and the challenge were. A chaplain will often engage with individuals and groups for short periods of time, they will build on short-term contacts, but eventually let people fade back into the school population. There will be few tasks that keep the chaplain focused on one group for long periods. Instead the chaplain will always be starting, engaging, meeting needs and then letting people go. There is an ascetism in this challenge of *letting go* that keeps the chaplain flexible in meeting needs and free from the politics of small groups in the school.

Chapter Two
Starting a Chaplaincy

Planning an appointment

A school that has decided in principle that it wishes to appoint a chaplain is in a unique position to renew or re-focus its ethos and spiritual life as a Gospel community. In the process of planning and recruiting a chaplain there is also potential to increase the depth of knowledge and clarity around spirituality within the governing body and the leadership groups in the school. Appointing a chaplain has many features that will be similar to the appointment of any other staff member in terms of process, contracts and issues such as equal opportunity. However, some elements of a chaplain's appointment introduce questions and possibilities not usually provoked by other appointments:

- There is no single recognised qualification for chaplaincy - what kind of qualification is appropriate?[9]

- Salary scales are not clear.

- A wider variety of skills and experience is demanded by chaplaincy and the role itself can be viewed, with varying levels of status, within the hierarchy of the school.

- Initial job descriptions are inevitably vague since much will depend upon the relationship skills and strengths of the appointee.

- The package of support for chaplaincy needs to go beyond line-management to informal supervision[10] and to the provision of personal retreats in some contracts.

- Evaluation of the work of chaplaincy is difficult and performance targets are not easy to set.[11]

These differences make the appointment of a chaplain an opportunity to think about the role in a different way and use the planning process to clarify with the whole-school community what kind of chaplaincy is needed. The guide produced by the Catholic Education Service (CES) for the employment of lay chaplains offers a clear description of the process that will make these appointments safe.[12]

---

[9] These might include a degree in theology, counselling and teaching qualifications, social work qualifications, lay reader or catechist training, qualification in the health professions and youth work qualifications. The field is wide and usually the chaplain will have already held a professional post in another discipline.
[10] See chapter eight for more detail.
[11] See chapter seven for a variety of models for chaplaincy evaluation.
[12] *Guide to Employment of Lay Chaplains in Schools & Colleges*, (London CES 2004).

The guide emphasises, on page five, that the appointment needs to be tailored to the specific needs of the school, then the personnel specification and job description will harmonise with the perceived needs of the school community. Advertising for a chaplain needs more thought than that of a teaching post because many of the best candidates may well be in other professions, with skills that can be transferred into chaplaincy with additional training. The Catholic Gazette is an under-used resource as a way of reaching potential candidates and the *Ad Clerum* newsletter to parish priests can also be accessed to raise awareness in the faith community of chaplaincy roles. The Association of Catholic Chaplains in Education has a website that can help circulate information on available posts.[13] Some schools have found the local press and *The Big Issue* to be useful ways of reaching a larger population of professionals with skills that can be transferred, with additional training, into chaplaincy roles. There are links to training available in the resources at the end of this book.

Different models of chaplaincy

The Bishop of Salisbury, at a recent meeting of secondary heads, made the following comment,

> Each school is different and the spiritual needs of the youngsters requires a bespoke chaplaincy model which suits local circumstances.[14]

Each school, therefore, needs to create its own model of chaplaincy that reflects the unique pattern of needs and traditions that will shape the focus of the chaplain's work. The local situation will also affect the extent to which the chaplain will be expected to work in partnership within the school and with other agencies beyond the school site.

Some basic options need to be clarified about the preferred way of working for a school chaplain. Below are a few of the options a school might like to consider in the process of preparing for an appointment. They are presented to provoke thought and are not in any way exhaustive of the possibilities that might make up a *bespoke* chaplaincy.

1 A full-time co-ordinating lay chaplain

This type of chaplain is expected to draw from the school community the

---

[13] The website can be found at http://www.acce.org.uk
[14] *Diocese of Salisbury Schools Meeting* Nov 7th 2007 Bishop David Stancliffe.

skills and commitment to provide a wide range of chaplaincy provision. It is a useful role to adopt in a school where there are many skills in the existing staff, already providing a large amount of chaplaincy provision. Appointing this kind of chaplain allows their work to continue, to be supported and resourced effectively. It allows the school to draw upon its traditions and integrate existing commitment into the future.

The person needed for this role will generally have a wide experience of working alongside teaching staff and understand the pressures and possibilities of school structures. They will be good at inspiring, delegating and planning alongside senior colleagues in school.

2 A full-time chaplain responding largely to the needs of the young

If a school feels that it has its greatest chaplaincy challenge in specific needs among the students and already has a well-developed spiritual support programme for staff, it may wish to consider appointing a chaplain who is capable of working energetically with small groups and especially in extended hours beyond the curriculum. This kind of chaplaincy will be similar to youth ministry and has the flexibility to work alongside parish programmes and support a wide range of liturgy and extra-curricular activity.

The candidate for this type of chaplaincy would need to have high levels of energy, creativity and relationship skills. They would need very active and detailed line-management to avoid clashes with school patterns and personal burn-out.

3 A full-time chaplaincy team leader alongside named staff

A school may wish to appoint a full-time chaplain but also appoint some members of staff for specific periods of time to work together and establish a consistent chaplaincy provision across all age groups on the school site. The advantage of having paid part-time members of staff and not volunteers is that it gives the leadership a greater control and accountability for chaplaincy. From the chaplain's viewpoint this partnership is seen as supportive and can help maintain a wider view of the needs of the school and continuity should the chaplain move on to other work.

This kind of chaplain needs collaborative skills too and especially communication skills to maintain patterns of provision with busy staff.

4   Using existing staff

Some schools have seconded teaching staff to maintain a chaplaincy during part of their working week. This is a model that many existing chaplains find difficult to manage because it can lead to some role conflict when the kind of relationship, a class teacher needs to maintain, clashes with the different boundaries established in a chaplaincy role. Secondly, the availability of a full-time dedicated chaplain is a clear statement to the school community of the value of the spiritual dimension in school life. The chaplain is an embodiment of that value and the witness to that value is severely reduced when the chaplain has another role which will often be seen as *their real job*. However, as a stepping stone towards a full-time chaplaincy such a secondment can be a useful interim stage.

These models are not exhaustive nor mutually exclusive. They are listed mainly to provoke the kind of discussion that will lead to the *bespoke chaplaincy* mentioned by the Bishop of Salisbury. The levels of skills and experience required in these models vary greatly and the need for support and guidance, especially early on, will also vary. Appointing a chaplain who is under-skilled is only appropriate if support and training can be provided in adequate amounts. The field of potential candidates for such roles may also be patchy and selection may seem very risky, especially if the school is making its first appointment in this area.

The focus of chaplaincy

The breadth of needs addressed by chaplaincy is at once a challenge and a blessing. The breadth of needs represented in an average secondary school and the potential of students for growth and spiritual development is huge. Unless the school plans for the kind of chaplain it needs, the appointee will not have enough focus to be effective or enough agreed targets to feel that success has been achieved. However, each chaplain has specific gifts, experience, energies and interests which would also shape the final job description that eventually emerges after an appointment. The school however, needs to be clear about how it sees its needs and what priorities it has for a chaplain to address. Below is a list of six areas identified in the CES guidelines as broad areas of chaplaincy that a school may wish to reflect upon as it prepares for the appointment of a chaplain. Parish and neighbourhood links have been added to the list to bring it to particular prominence which I have added as a seventh broad area. Each of these areas will overlap with one another but they provide useful focal points for reflection.

1 Spiritual accompaniment

A chaplain is asked to *walk* with people, sometimes over long periods, in a spiritual relationship that is close to, but different from, counselling. It implies a focus on individual needs that can mean being a cheerful presence around school, remembering names, to more intensive accompaniment through life-changes with staff or issues, like bereavement, with students. The ability to listen, to share feelings and to be still is a vital part of this accompaniment role as is a familiarity with the scripture, tradition and liturgies of the Church. There are courses available in spiritual direction that are relevant as qualifications for chaplaincy applicants or for professional development after employment.[15]

2 Pastoral Care

The ability to relate to a wide range of individuals and establish levels of trust where problems can be shared is a key skill for the pastoral dimension of chaplaincy. The focus on the marginalised and at risk members of the school community is rooted in a preferential option for the poor that has been part of Church concern for the last two decades. The chaplain working with pastoral needs has to be extremely clear about how the chaplaincy works alongside the main pastoral provision of the school and maintain the same protocols, especially about recording events and contact with students' parents or guardians. The ability of the chaplain to support those who bear the burden of pastoral care and discipline is especially important. Induction of a chaplain should include specific information about child protection guidelines and procedures and ways of referring young people effectively within the school and beyond.

3 Evangelisation

The need to have the Gospel lived and witnessed to in the ordinary life of the school is a principle part of chaplaincy provision. The chaplain is there to help people to pray, to recognise the love of God in present patterns in the school and to help put flesh on the stories of scripture that are reflected in the daily experience of classrooms and playgrounds. Chaplains achieve this work of evangelisation through creating small groups for prayer, social justice and reflection. They evangelise through whole-school events such as family fast days and encouraging participation in planned liturgies. Identifying leaders and training them to be peer leaders can help bring the Gospel to life in the school community.

---

[15] A first step to research training would be to contact the Retreat Movement for a listing of ongoing training in spiritual direction. www.retreats.org.uk

4 Catechesis

A chaplain is expected to support the growth of individuals and groups into full membership of the Church when appropriate. In some dioceses the preparation for confirmation provides a significant moment to do this each year. Individuals may also be accompanied by the chaplain through the rites of initiation with the permission of their parish priest. Even those who are full members of the Church may benefit from further reflection and development provided by programmes such as CaFE[16] and Catholic Alpha courses. In addition, a chaplain will be expected to support the provision of retreats of different types for a wide range of groups through the school.

5 Religious Education

The chaplain is expected to support and extend the work of the Religious Education department in the school. The specialist staff in that department have specific skills that can also support the work of the chaplain. The collaboration of chaplain and Religious Education department can be especially rich when instruction within the curriculum can be extended into related experience through chaplaincy provision. Therefore, when justice and peace, or prayer, or worship is being studied, the chaplain can help to provide extension experiences that support the curriculum. If this area is seen as vital to a chaplain's role, the Religious Education department will need a significant part in the preparation and selection of the candidates. However, it is important to remember that the chaplain is not part of a department or line-managed through another department. The chaplain has a whole-school remit and needs accountability at the level of whole-school management.

6 Liturgical Celebration

The identity of the school as a Church school is experienced most visibly when the school celebrates liturgy and prays together. The preparation and planning of these celebrations is another focal point for chaplaincy. The chaplain needs to draw large areas of the school life into major celebrations to maximise participation and to ensure that the liturgy is conducted with appropriate dignity and depth. The provision of support for voluntary liturgies, for classroom prayers and for assembly support as well as staff prayer moments is also part of this role. There should be a liturgy statement in the school documentation outlining clearly what the basic minimum of prayer, liturgy and other celebrations are for the whole school and different

---

[16] Catholic Faith Exploration.

groups within the school community. A strong liturgical dimension to chaplaincy demands a confident and creative chaplain with good animation and collaborative skills. Those gifts will ensure that staff and pupils are drawn into the creation of resources for collective worship and events that feed the spiritual life of the school.

7 Parish and neighbourhood liaison

The visible school community is not the only focal point for school chaplaincy. Parents, past pupils and parishes are obvious and first-hand links into the local community. In some areas, strong parental networks can demand large amounts of commitment. In other areas, deanery youth and catechetical projects may need regular support from the school chaplain. The network of PTA and past pupils may be seen by the school as an untapped resource that a chaplain could access on behalf of the whole-school community. Liaison with other Churches and links with ecumenical and inter-faith networks could be a vital component of chaplaincy.

Reviewing these seven areas in the light of the needs of a specific school and with some preference for the model of chaplaincy that fits the school, should help to focus the minds of those planning for the appointment of a chaplain and to get the most out of the CES guidelines already mentioned.

Budgeting

It seems obvious to assume that a chaplain will have a budget with which to work but I have known a number of schools who have no assigned budget for their chaplains, expecting them to ask for every specific need. Sometimes they are allowed to draw upon the reprographics quotas of other departments or are sent to ask for resources from other departments. This situation is obviously unhelpful and yet establishing a budget at the start of a chaplaincy may be quite difficult. Models of financial management vary and the amount of flexibility in the overall budget will vary too. However, to commit to the employment of a chaplain is to commit to resourcing them as well. In assigning an initial budget to the post the school needs to consider how the chaplain will work and how quickly they wish them to get into action. Most schools operate a budget from April and therefore typical appointments in September will only have half a financial year in which to survive. For a new chaplain, as will be seen later, half of that time may be spent in establishing relationships in and around the school and running some provisional activities before proposing a more comprehensive plan that can be negotiated more accurately into an April budget. Upon induction, the chaplain should, at a minimum, be given a nominal budget to cover any immediate costs involved in hospitality, liturgy, resourcing and travel.

A chaplaincy has a range of financial needs for its day-to-day running which have to be met as part of its core activity in relation to the school. These would include:

- Hospitality - coffee, tea, mugs, kettle etc. After 6 months, donations can cover this, chaplains are also expected to manage visitors and have handouts and resources that can promote the spirit of the school.

- Reprographics - Sufficient copying quantities for a small department and a number of whole-school events.

- Display materials - Paper, card, glue, pins, staplers, laminates etc.

- Liturgical resources - Books, assembly resources, candles, hosts, music.

- Travel - A chaplain will need a mileage reclaim facility.

Non-managerial supervision costs[17]

These core items of the chaplain's work will need to be consistently present in any budget. The rest of the budget needs to be negotiated with the school as part of the planning stage. If the plan involves provision of retreat experiences off-site then venue and travel costs need to be built in at the planning stage. If a chaplaincy plan demands a lot of liturgical development, some training elements might attract significant costs which could draw on the staff-development budget. If there is a strong pastoral element to the chaplaincy some subsidy for certain events might also need to be incorporated into a budget. Therefore, after the initial start-up period for a chaplaincy a school needs to estimate what the core costs are and then, year by year, invite the chaplain to draw up detailed costs of an annual action plan, within the normal planning routine of the school. The additions to the budget beyond the core costs could then be project-based for that year only and not assumed to continue year-on-year as happens in some schools. The busier the chaplaincy becomes, the more expense it will incur. Evaluating the effectiveness of the chaplaincy must therefore include the financial cost as an important element and *value for money* is an issue that is still legitimate, even in the less well-defined aims of chaplaincy.

---

[17] See chapter eight for more details on this subject.

Some start-up costs need to be budgeted for at the beginning of a chaplaincy role. Such items as a computer, furniture, telephone, materials to make a warm drink for visitors and on large school sites a pager or a mobile phone can all help to make the chaplain more available and effective in the first few months. A final element of chaplaincy finance is fundraising. Much of the fundraising done by chaplaincy is rightly focused on specific campaigns and around the issues of justice and peace. However, it is also helpful for chaplains to invite members of the school community to raise funds for specific projects that help to build ownership of the chaplaincy by the whole community. Our chaplaincy has grown immeasurably through the donation of furniture, plants for our peace garden and donations towards a conservatory for counselling provision. The involvement of the wider community in these in-school projects achieves some of the aims of chaplaincy whilst easing the budget burden on the school generally. Therefore, when reviewing requests for funding around chaplaincy, it is useful from time to time to go cap in hand to others to give them the chance to support and own the developments in chaplaincy that are usually provided as added value items in a Church school.

A Chaplaincy Base

I know one school chaplain who was appointed to the post without being given a base to work from. He survived for six months before resigning. Whilst much of the chaplain's work can be achieved on the school corridors and playground, a base is still essential. Providing a base is a statement by the school that chaplaincy exists, has status and permanence within the school. The kind of base that is established will depend upon the available space and the vision of chaplaincy that the school is proposing. Some schools are happy to see the chaplain as a counsellor and pastoral worker who could work adequately from a small room where interviews, administration and resourcing can happen. Other chaplaincy plans may require the chaplain to work with small groups, maintain a high level of hospitality and create a social space where an informal atmosphere prevails through the day. Such an approach would imply the commitment of a classroom sized space with some investment into softer furnishing and atmosphere. Other bases might take the form of a small prayer room with some space for administration. Whatever space is assigned to the chaplain, it will inevitably begin to shape the chaplain's way of working and will project an image of the value and scope of chaplaincy to the rest of the school.

The decision about the location of the chaplaincy base needs to be considered in the light of the chaplaincy priorities of the school. Proximity to the Religious

Education department will be an advantage where a catechetical model of working is dominant. In a more pastoral model, closeness to the year-leaders or mentor bases would make more sense. For a prayer room style of base, the quieter corridors in the school would need to be considered first. If the school is fortunate enough to have a chapel, then a chaplaincy base close by would be appropriate. The ability to access the chaplain in a quiet space directly from the playground has always been seen as advantageous.

The chaplaincy base is a place to find the chaplain, to leave messages and to meet the chaplain for various activities. It is not a place that contains the chaplain's work. Much of the chaplain's role is achieved through the informal and accidental meetings on corridors, in the flexibility to spend time with individual needs and support specific initiatives and respond to urgent needs on and away from the school site. The chaplaincy base will therefore not have the intensity of use that other rooms may have. In a school with room pressures it is important to maintain the dedicated nature of this base as far as possible because the atmosphere and intent behind the work that goes on in the room is different: it is informal, based on listening before learning and the area needs to be seen as sacred space. The root of the word sacred actually means consecrated – set apart. A school that can provide this dedicated space is making a spiritual statement about the values of the school. To use it for other purposes such as for disciplining, exam invigilation will undermine the impact the base has in the school context.

Starting work with a lay chaplain

The CES guidelines outline a good structure of induction that includes:

- Compiling an information pack on the school.

- Providing an annotated list of staff with roles that link to the chaplain's role.

- Providing a plan of the site and buildings.

- Talking through the staff handbook and identifying key policies to be highlighted.

- Indicating key diary events for the chaplain to be aware of or to attend or prepare.

The first week

Beginning a new school for any adult is challenging. For a chaplain, when the role is so broad and the support structures are so different from other school departments the experience can be overwhelming. The chaplain, beginning in September, will be joining the school amongst a flurry of new beginnings without the anchor of a clearly defined role. Their greatest need will be for reassurance and some clear information about their role and the first steps. A newly arrived chaplain should be given a timetable of structured experiences that will cover about a third of each school day. The other two thirds should be left unstructured for the chaplain to begin their work of building informal contacts and listening for needs.

The first week's timetable might include things like:

- The normal welcome, briefing and training events for all staff within which the chaplain should be mentioned as available for pupils and for staff.

- Shadowing a specific member of staff on the first or second day so that support and the rhythm of the day is picked up quickly.

- A structured walk around the whole-school site by the site manager who could give a broad based view of the whole school.

- The chance to be in the playground at each break and lunch time.

- A walk around the school with an articulate student or a small group who can explain the best and the worst elements of the school site.

- An invitation to sit in a range of specific classes later in the week to cover a range of subjects and age groups. This could be achieved through shadowing a support assistant or a student for part of their day.

- A chance to meet the Chair of Governors.

- A specific conversation with the child protection officer about procedures and any specific issues about one-to-one working with young people.

- A specific meeting with the line-manager to clarify resourcing the role.

- An invitation to work with a member of staff on the preparation of opening services or prayers for the school year.

A chaplain might be encouraged to keep a daily diary of first impressions and any initial ideas about opportunities for developing chaplaincy. This might last for a few weeks or for the whole first term and become a resource for supervision as well as planning.

The first week might end with a feedback session with the headteacher or the line-manager of the chaplain. The chaplain will need time to read, establish their base and absorb a lot of information. They need to be encouraged to walk the school and feel free to introduce themselves in offices, canteens and informal groupings in the staff room.

The first month

The aim of the first month is to identify the broad spiritual needs of the school and to absorb the views and the hopes of a wide range of the school community. In order to achieve this awareness a chaplain would benefit from a series of structured conversations with a range of stakeholders in the school community. The list might include some of the following: a governor of the school, key senior staff, the head of RE, members of the administration staff, the school bursar, a small group of articulate pupils, a group of parents engaged with the school, some past pupils, a member of the local clergy[18] and another local chaplain linked into the diocesan chaplaincy network. The structure of the conversation should include some basic questions about how these people experience the school community, what are the greatest spiritual needs of the school and what spiritual strengths they recognise at present. The conversations can also be helped by the chaplain being aware of the basic literature already sent out to parents and students.

The purpose of all this listening is to help the chaplain gain an in-depth knowledge of the school quickly and begin the process of establishing a long-term plan in partnership with senior staff in the school. The results of these conversations should be noted in a diary and used as background for planning. Whilst this longer term listening takes place the chaplain needs to engage in some direct tasks with young people and a specific timetable should be established for a series of one-off events that will introduce the chaplain and the chaplaincy to a range of pupils. One chaplain managed this by taking a small group from named Religious Education classes for some meditation exercises. In the process of a short experience she was able to work informally and make

---

[18] Sometime in the first three months, a chaplain might be introduced to the local deanery meeting of clergy to explore any possible plans for ministry they might have and identify how a school chaplaincy might support such plans.

herself known to a wide range of students in an area where she felt very confident.

In the first month the chaplain needs to meet with any groups that overlap with chaplaincy: environmental groups, schools councils, fair trade, CAFOD, SVP, choir groups, mediation groups, support groups, bereavement groups and so on. These groups and the staff that lead them will be key supporters of chaplaincy in the future. In the first month the chaplain will also begin to notice gaps in the school provision and gaps in their own knowledge. Some chaplains have instituted a school-wide survey that asked the simple question, *What do you want your chaplain to do, for your year group, for staff and for the whole school?* This formal enquiry creates the opportunity for the chaplain to open up a dialogue with the whole school and, in the process, emphasise the needs-led nature of much chaplaincy work.

By the end of the first month the chaplain should have had some specific experiences and time to listen and to feedback early impressions to the whole school. The chaplain needs to establish credibility with staff and pupils as a competent professional in working pastorally, spiritually, safely and creatively with a wide range of needs. At the end of the month the chaplain should have time for an extended line-management meeting and chance to block out the rest of the term in some specific planning that will lead to a more structured role for the rest of the term. After that session the chaplain should then be ready for a session of non-managerial supervision.

At some point, after the probationary period is complete, a school may wish to formally induct their chaplain into the school. An induction ceremony is highly recommended for headteachers but can also apply to the role of chaplain because it is a unique role of spiritual leadership within the community. An induction emphasises the service dimension of the chaplain's role and the sacred nature of their ministry. For lay chaplains especially the induction can provide the mandate and commissioning that they need from the whole community to act as a minister of the Church. The induction ceremony should involve a wide range of the community expressing their hopes and expectations with a presentation of some Christian symbols. At some point in this ceremony, the chaplain should also make a promise. In large schools, where it is not possible to gather the whole school, an assembly-style induction service can be devised for each year group.[19]

---

[19] Some resources are available from an induction service in Salesian College Battersea at www.salesians.org.uk/chap

Chapter Three
Linking with Leadership

In general, chaplaincy should not be seen to be part of the hierarchy of the school; however it should be a role with status and, above all else, influence. Association with the decision-making process of the school should be clearly one of pastoral care and Gospel vision. A chaplain who becomes a member of the governing body, effectively becomes the employer of every adult in the school and could lose some freedom to relate to staff members in the process. A chaplain who is part of a management team may be drawn into detailed aspects of planning and discipline that might compromise the more pastoral aspects of a chaplain's role. It is better not to present chaplains with those dilemmas, but leave them free to operate informally and for the good of the whole school through the influence and inspiration of others.

The Headteacher

Establishing a good relationship with the headteacher is a crucial foundation for the chaplain in school. There is a need for regular meetings and informal contact between a headteacher and the chaplain so that information and opinions can be exchanged in a safe forum. One of the greatest gifts a chaplain brings to a school is a silence and confidentiality that allows people to speak freely. This freedom and safety to speak is a valuable asset for any headteacher. As a leader in the school they may be caught up in the politics of promotions and budgets in a way that leads them to be very careful in communicating even with close colleagues. The chaplain can provide a conversation which is almost confessional in its secrecy and allow the headteacher to rehearse thoughts and options with someone who knows the school well but is not immediately tied into the decision making process. This role demands a large degree of maturity and integrity from the chaplain and it is a role that has to be earned over time by the chaplain and not to be assumed as part of the role. Such confidentiality needs to be considered as part of the detailed contractual standards of a chaplain.

Once a good relationship has been established, the chaplain can be a source of personal support to the headteacher at stressful times. The opportunity for the chaplain to challenge will grow, with the confidence the headteacher brings to the relationship. At times, the chaplain might need to spell out the Gospel implications of some decisions and keep the ethos of the school high in the agenda of the headteacher. At other times the head will be able to challenge the chaplain to make the ethos more evident in school or to support particular members of staff in need. The effect of a regular conversation with the headteacher allows the chaplain to reinforce the headteacher as the spiritual leader of the school and the first witness to the Gospel and the life of the spirit.

Another aspect of this regular and confidential exchange is that it allows the chaplain to share a view of the *shadow side* of the school. The chaplain has the privilege of being around to listen to people in any part of the school. A good chaplain walks the school as a prayerful pilgrimage each day stopping as people engage in conversation and waiting to observe the normal ebb and flow of corridors and classrooms. This leads the chaplain to gather a view of the informal side of the school. The deeper emotions, opinions, energy and dreams of a school community are rarely expressed in meetings and in documents but they stand in the shadow of the issues a school must deal with every day. This backdrop to the school's life is influential in making or breaking the plans of the school community and the routines that make up each day. The chaplain absorbs this shadow side of the school, the unspoken and the hidden feelings of staff and pupils and can bring that shadow side into a regular exchange with the headteacher without ever betraying any confidences since any comments made by the chaplain would be the result of multiple opinions and impressions built up over time. Reading this shadow side of the school can help headteachers to be more responsive and aware of the school life and hence better able to manage the school in the light of the Gospel.

Another aspect of this conversation with the head is that some basic information can be shared from beyond the school for the benefit of the whole community. The chaplain, alongside other colleagues, has the task of linking the work of the school into local parishes, deanery, pastoral areas and dioceses. Information can be taken both ways by the chaplain and pastoral opportunities can be identified for links between pupils and parishes. Similar ecumenical and neighbourhood links can be brought into this discussion to help the school remain integrated into the local community as a witness to Gospel values.

The Governing Body

The governing body of a school is a vital part of the long-term and sometimes day-to-day running of the school. The governors are volunteers with a wide variety of backgrounds and many different levels of knowledge and expertise about schools. The governors are also the employers of staff in many voluntary aided schools and therefore have statutory rights to hire and fire and maintain contractual obligations with staff, including the management of disciplinary matters with teachers and pupils. It is better for a chaplain not to be involved

---

[19] Some resources are available from an induction service in Salesian College Battersea at www.salesians.org.uk/chap

directly in this aspect of the governing of the school since, at times, the interests of the chaplain's pastoral role and statutory role may divide. Some members of staff, knowing that a chaplain is a governor, will regard this as a barrier and in times of dispute the neutrality of the chaplain and the ability to mediate becomes eroded. This does not mean that the chaplain cannot take part in specific discussions and bring the influence of chaplaincy to bear on certain areas of governance.

The ethos committee and the staffing committee are possible areas where the chaplain might make a welcome contribution from time to time. In some schools there is a standing group that searches for new members of the governing body to which a chaplain may be able to make a valued contribution. The chaplain should also find access to the governors to provide prayers, reflections, information on possible candidates for governance and periodic reports on the work of the chaplaincy. Where appropriate the chaplain should also be encouraged to provide specific training for governors in the area of ethos and spirituality.

Another way that the chaplain can establish links with the governing body is by creating easy opportunities for them to access the school during its working day. The chaplaincy base can provide a venue for small groups to meet governors. Small presentations and events can trigger invitations and the chaplain can host these visits because of the flexibility their role creates. In a similar way, the opportunity for pupils and staff to recognise and celebrate the work that the governors do for the school can be achieved through chaplaincy in discussion with the headteacher. The chaplain can also make a point of inviting governors to all liturgical events through clear diary planning and specific invitations to come and celebrate. In some schools a governor, who has the time, has been incorporated into the chaplaincy team.

Chaplaincy in the planning framework

Within the school a chaplaincy might need to adopt the shape of a department if it is to gain the recognition it needs to grow within the school community. It will need to establish its aims, objectives, targets and budget with a clarity that mirrors that of other departments and yet retain a flexibility needed to achieve its aims. Like any other department it needs to be evaluated and, like any other staff member, a chaplain needs line-management and appraisal. Evaluating chaplaincy is considered in chapter seven.

The rhythm of planning in a school should not exclude chaplaincy as a special case. It helps if chaplaincy can establish its credentials as a related but different discipline alongside other departments. Therefore the publishing of plans, establishment of targets and regular accountability for outcomes and budgets should apply to chaplaincy as a part of a broad-based service for young people. The discipline involved in chaplaincy is that of non-formal work with people of all ages in school. It has a process that begins with individual needs and moves to small groups in order to heal, celebrate and sustain the wider community. The curriculum is not set down in advance but negotiated in an educative conversation with many people. Because the curriculum emerges through relationships it can adapt and change through the planning year. Therefore, a more reflective and flexible form of planning should be at work in the background of a chaplaincy. That does not mean that chaplaincy should not be planned! It does mean that more space needs to be planned into time scales and there should be an expectation that plans may change, not through whim or because of apathy, but by the change and development of the relationships that make up a school community.

One reason why planning in a chaplaincy needs more flexibility is because it is based on an exploratory model of education. The curriculum for informal educators is not fixed. Flexibility to the needs, of the individual and the group, demands that there are fewer fixed points. That will allow scope for adaptation and a different type of skill from the chaplain in managing time and targets. The planning behind chaplaincy can be very detailed for the first few steps. After that, once a group has begun or feedback has been received, the viewpoint may also have changed. There may be new possibilities emerging or some key people who volunteered prove unwilling to persevere. Another critical factor in chaplaincy work is that most plans are built upon the goodwill of volunteers among staff, pupils and parents. That goodwill can change and sometimes evaporate entirely in one day. Space is needed to keep working slowly at chaplaincy plans to gain and sustain commitment from very busy people. A chaplaincy that tries to mirror the frantic pace of work in a typical secondary school is not doing its job. The chaplaincy cannot achieve its basic aim of being present and pointing to the Gospel if it is too busy to listen to individuals and groups in school. One way of looking at a chaplaincy plan is to see it as a way of balancing fixed time with flexible time so that there is always some element of both in each day.

The process of teaching and learning that goes on in every classroom also happens in chaplaincy. Instead of lessons a chaplain has conversations. Instead of exercises and tests a chaplain has group experiences. At the end of the classroom experiences a school hopes that each pupil has a love or at least a grasp of that subject to a good level. At the end of a chaplaincy experience the chaplain hopes that the young person has a grasp of the mystery and dignity of their own lives and the lives of others and the way that the Gospel makes sense of all of life. Planning for each of these settings may look very different but the chaplaincy and the classroom are both sacred places of teaching and learning by different processes both of which lead to the development of the whole child.

Informed and Consulted

Having argued that the chaplain needs to be somewhat peripheral and a special case in terms of leadership and planning it is important to assert that a good chaplain needs to be informed and consulted on major issues within the school community. The chaplain has a privileged view of the school community that may be unique in its scope and depth. This view will be conditioned by a chaplain's personality, age, gender and their level of involvement in the day-to-day activity of the school. The chaplain will have access to a wide spectrum of hopes, fears and even prejudices that have been absorbed in countless conversations and a habit of observing and reflecting on life in school.

This reflective watching and listening, on the part of the chaplain, opens up the shadow side of the school mentioned earlier. It is important that this view is recognised, in decision-making, by the school not only to promote better decisions but also to determine how and when those decisions might best be implemented. A chaplain who is not consulted informally by the school is an unused asset that could save much wasted energy and heartache in the implementing of change. In a similar way, the leadership groups in the school could benefit by keeping the chaplain informed of their ongoing plans so that a chaplain can help clarify and promote a positive attitude to change. The ability of staffroom chatter to move from news of a leadership decision to a conspiracy theory can be very rapid. The ability of a chaplain to understand the motives behind any change can help to ease the tension and the uncertainty generated in some staff.

Behind the informal flow of information through the chaplain is a discipline of concern and confidentiality that can help to ease and adapt change to the pace and needs of the school. The treasure that the chaplain brings to this information exchange is the Gospel context where the change is recognised not simply as a policy issue but rather as a process of growth in a living Christian community. In the context of the Gospel all the tough and challenging decisions a school has to make are transformed into acts of love that have a deeper meaning. The chaplain is a focal point where plans and information can be revealed as acts of faith in life and Gospel expressions of care for people in the school community. One of the skills a chaplain needs is the ability to translate Gospel values into the language of a secularised culture and thereby opening up the spiritual energy and sense of community that is implicit in many educational plans.

Spiritual leadership in the curriculum

Christians believe that the creative touch of God extends into all creation and especially to people made in God's image. Therefore, each area of curriculum from science to sociology will create opportunities to engage with the spiritual dimension of life. From the mystery of the origins of the universe in science to the wonder of human love explored in the humanities, Christians recognise a common story that holds these things together and gives meaning to the whole of life. The chaplain needs to be available to those who plan and deliver the curriculum to identify the points where the spiritual dimension rises to the surface in their subject area and becomes more explicit. Helping subject leaders recognise the sacred as well as the pragmatic benefits of their subject is a task that the chaplain should be well prepared to achieve.

Once areas of spiritual interest are identified, the subject leaders may be able to develop some learning experiences that can lead directly into reflection, discussion or even into meditation and silence within the curriculum. The movement of the earth and the expanse of time outlined in physical geography can lead to a breathtaking perspective on our short life and its meaning. Likewise, the patterns that arise from mathematics or the exploration of character and human frailty in English novels can unearth profound questions in many young lives. Ofsted[20] produced an excellent document on the evaluation of the spiritual dimension of schools and encouraged teaching styles which could:

> encourage pupils to relate their learning to a wider frame of reference – for example, asking 'why?', 'how?' and 'where?' as well as 'what?'[21]

---

[20] The Office for Standards in Education in England and Wales
[21] Promoting and evaluating pupils' spiritual, moral, social and cultural development. (HMI March 2004).

One school has stimulated reflection on the links between spirituality and curriculum by adding a question to the annual departmental review. The question simply asks how well the ethos is promoted in their department. The annual rhythm of asking this question stimulates connections and raises awareness of spiritual dimension in all of school life. The chaplain who can draw the spiritual out of the secular can help teachers to proclaim the Gospel in every classroom and in every subject. The impact of international trade in geography might be linked into a fair trade issue by a chaplain. The issue of holocaust in history might lead to a chaplain celebrating holocaust memorial day in school. The issue of social justice might trigger a CAFOD group being generated through the chaplaincy in school. Raising deep questions in any subject and allowing a mystery to be explored before answers are reached allows the wounded imagination of the young to grow into wonder. The chaplain needs to be a trusted colleague, widely read and able to make deep connections between questions of life and faith. A superficial or narrow faith will not do for the chaplain.

Chapter Four
Chaplaincy
&
Pastoral Care

A chaplain is not primarily a social worker or a counsellor, even though they may have the skills and, at times, operate in these types of roles. A chaplain is not a disciplinarian nor solely concerned with the staff or pupils most at risk in the school community. A chaplain is primarily a minister of the Gospel within the school and works as a visible sign of the school's commitment to an integrated spiritual life for all the school community. It is easy for a school to use the chaplain only as a friendly and skilled support for the pastoral provision of the school. The chaplain has much more than that to offer and has a variety of roles in the many different models of pupil support in school.

Pastoral systems in schools vary greatly in their reach and in their status. In a Christian context, the link between pastoral care and the Gospel should be strong and clear; consequently pastoral support should have a high profile and status. The root of the word *pastoral* is found in the role of the shepherd who guards and guides the flock. In particular, the shepherd seeks out and rescues the lost and reconnects them with the other sheep. This description, captured in chapter ten of John's Gospel, outlines the importance of safe places, identifying threats before they happen and celebrating the achievement of individuals. The richness of this term is more eloquent than the term *pupil support*, which does not have the depth and richness of the word *pastoral*.

The *year tutor or learning mentor* is therefore a spiritual figure in the school, living the Gospel in the daily pattern of their work. They identify the lost sheep, they draw people into groups, and they bind up the wounded and carry the weak and vulnerable to safe places. The chaplain's role is to support this spiritual dimension of their work and help them to sustain the toll it can sometimes take on their patience and their emotions. The chaplain is not simply another flexible helper for those involved in pastoral care, but a specialist in the informal art of linking life and faith, through protecting and promoting the dignity of each person.

At times, chaplains may be drawn to support specific pastoral needs and may be a crucial link in crisis situations because of their experience and the spiritual dimension they have to offer. The aim of the chaplain is to work alongside the pastoral staff as a colleague and not to do their job for them. The pastoral staff need to see the chaplain as one type of referral among many that they can make for a pupil. The best person to deal with a bereavement situation, for example, may not be the chaplain at all but a form tutor who knows the family well. The chaplain in that situation can provide resources to the supporter, giving information about bereavement, about funerals, about readings for funerals. The chaplain can help with the issues of personal support from other pupils.

The chaplain's role and personal skills are available for a wide range of contact with pupils and staff, opening up individual needs. The temptation could be for the chaplain to develop their own *clientele* and a pattern of guidance that parallels rather than integrates with the pastoral system. Part of the professionalism of the chaplain includes the discipline of keeping appropriate records and communicating clearly about conversations with specific pupils. A chaplain's pastoral work needs to be harmonised with broader pastoral care in the school. Some pupils seem to be able to attract the pastoral attention of a number of key staff and even play one off against the other in an unhelpful way. Communication between colleagues is vital in avoiding such misuse of valuable time and resources.

For most purposes, the chaplain should regard the pastoral conversation as a referral from the pastoral provision of the school, even if a pupil has referred themselves to the chaplain. Some information and a note about ongoing conversations with the chaplain should be recorded within the pastoral system. Those who have primary responsibility for the pastoral care of young people need to know which pupils are talking to the chaplain. The chaplain needs to be accountable for those conversations within the limits of normal confidentiality. For older students, some of this accountability needs to be more sensitive and muted as students move towards increased autonomy. The chaplain will always be required to work safely within the normal pattern set by the policies of a school.

Contact with pupils' families

Chaplaincy contacts with home must fit into an agreed pattern of school policy. The normal pattern of permissions and recording should apply to the chaplain, as to any other member of staff. For the safety of the chaplain and the good of the family, a chaplain needs to work closely with the year leaders. Families will not benefit from uncoordinated contact from the school. There will be times when the interests of individual pupils and the interests of the school may divide, not only on disciplinary issues but also on the more regular choices of options and school trips for example. In contacting the family, chaplains need to ensure that they are clear about their role and the limitations of their situation. They need to be sure of the facts and policies of the school, before speaking on behalf of the school community. As in many other chaplaincy situations, the challenge lies in reconciling some differences, but accepting necessary limits.

Discipline

One of the pastoral dilemmas of the chaplain is to know how far they can be drawn into disciplinary situations. In general, a chaplain needs to maintain an informal style in enforcing the rules of the school. This would include encouragement and reminders to keep the rules but does exclude becoming known as a *hard disciplinarian* in a way that repels some who may be the neediest pupils in school. Obviously no chaplain can ignore a serious incident in which young people or adults are being harmed. But should a chaplain confiscate a mobile phone being used in a classroom when the teacher is absent? Should a chaplain send a pupil to a senior staff member for persistently using bad language? These situations are not so clear. Showing disapproval or having a quiet word in the ear are both good informal methods of dealing with such behaviour that fit the role of the chaplain. However pursuing a situation where the chaplain has to impose their own sanctions, and operate through threat and fear is likely to undermine the chaplain's basic role.

Bereavement

The chaplaincy does have a specific role in the pastoral care of the bereaved and should generally be consulted if not directly involved in support. The bereavement may be a death in the family and the varying levels of distress that it may carry with it. Bereavement might also include the loss of a family in the separation of divorcing parents or even the onset of serious illness in a close family member. The processes of bereavement in either case raise spiritual issues, in an emotional context, that require sensitive skills and a faith-sensitive response.

Sometimes the most sensitive response is to do nothing more than promise the anonymous prayers of groups around the school and keep a careful watch on how the young person is coping. Raising the profile of someone who is suffering grief in school is not always the best pastoral approach and a quiet word can often be enough, in the early stages, to help a pupil cope. There will be time enough, later on, with self-chosen friends and adults, to allow the issues to arise at the pupil's own pace. Other pupils, with different personalities, will appreciate involvement from their friends, class groups and the general awareness of their situation being known in the school. In these settings, many questions about life, suffering and relationships will arise spontaneously and may draw the chaplain into discussion, reflection and prayer experiences with a variety of groups. The chaplain will have an expertise and connections into the local church that can help particularly at the time of the funeral and can advise on how pupils can become involved more effectively in the service.

The patterns of long-term response to bereavement are unique to each situation. The need to get back to normal for many young people is quite common and there may be reluctance for some time to raise the issue. For some, this period may extend to years and take the bereaved person beyond school age. For others, the emotional issues emerge either at home or in school, through behaviour or concentration difficulties. The chaplain can offer some support here because of their flexibility and the faith dimension of their role. They can also maintain some family links and encourage memory celebrations at anniversary dates or, in some families, even after the first month. The chaplain needs to ensure that a record is kept of the bereavement and the key dates in order to remind pastoral staff of these anniversary times, as they arise later. The chaplain will also be able to return to the young person regularly to offer the opportunity of further talk and to assess how they are coping. Chaplains may also be well placed to form small formal groups that can address this issue alongside caring adults in programmes such as *Seasons for Growth* and *Rainbows*.[22]

Small pastoral groups

Chaplaincy can make a huge contribution to the life of the school by helping to form small pastoral groups, aimed at helping others. These groups may involve staff and pupils together, or separately, living a gospel of service for others in the school community. The groups serve as visible links between the practical care offered by the school and the deeper spiritual values that motivate such care. Therefore a small anti-bullying group, organised by the pastoral staff, can be a focus for occasional reflection and prayer with the chaplain, about their work and the impact it is having on them. Other groups might be school councils, mission-statement drafting groups, or staff-support groups. It is important that the chaplain be invited into such groups to help make explicit links between their practical work and the spiritual dimension of such activity, based on the Gospel.

The chaplaincy should also offer these groups a venue for their meetings, a focal point for information, opportunities for training and the chance to network with similar groups within and beyond the school. The chaplain needs to maintain a strong interest in these groups because they act as *little churches* within the school where relationships are focused outward in service based on Gospel values. They can be described as visible signs of a deeper spirit within the school, where the Gospel comes into a sharper focus. Such groups extend the work of the

---

[22] See http://www.seasonsforgrowth.co.uk and http://www.rainbowsgb.org

pastoral system and the chaplaincy into parts of the school that normal provision cannot reach.

Caring for carers

The chaplain should be a daily visitor to those who provide specific pastoral care or pupil support within the school. The first reason for a daily visit is to exchange information that both the chaplain and the pastoral staff need to do their work. Pupil information, stories of events and incidents need to be exchanged so that the chaplain can consider an informal follow-up during the day ahead. The second reason for a regular visit to the pastoral teams in a school is to build up a strong working relationship with each of them. Many of the stresses and emotional burdens of a school are absorbed and carried in those who deal face-to-face with a range of pupil problems, though they may have little time and few resources to resolve the issues. Many pastoral staff are parents themselves and recognise, through their own parenting, the dilemmas of family life that young people live with each day.

The chaplain has a supportive role for each of these key people in school. The chaplains, simply because they are chaplains, can open up the deeper levels of motivation at work in pastoral staff and recognise the vocational dimension of their service to young people. In practical terms, the chaplain can be available for a chat, create a recovery space after a stressful event with a pupil and help staff to access prayer or support, as and when they need it. Above all, the chaplain can raise the profile and value of this vital role in a Christian school by recognising it in prayer, in reports, at meetings and in conversation with other staff members. The chaplain is one of the builders of an environment of care within a school community. That includes helping individuals to belong, to relax, to learn and to find meaning in their work. These four elements were part of the pastoral style of St John Bosco who is the patron of both youth and teachers.[23]

Form tutors

Form tutors are key partners for the chaplain in the school structure. These staff members are normally in daily contact with a group of about thirty pupils. Over a long period of time they will establish a body of knowledge, an opinion and a degree of care for each of them. In most schools it is they who lead the collective daily worship when it is not provided in a general assembly. They are

---

[23] For more on St John Bosco's approach see David O'Malley *Christian Leadership*, (Bolton Don Bosco Publications 2007).

first in importance in providing regular pastoral support. Their potential goes well beyond marking registers and checking organisers; they are the mood setters for the day and the voice of the school in that small group. Their attitudes and emotions can also make or break any initiatives presented to pupils by the chaplaincy.

This group requires recognition on a regular basis and some training, especially in the presentation of daily prayer in their classroom. They are expected to know the pupils in their group, not simply by name but in the story of their lives and in their personality. In each form group there is the potential to support one another, to encourage, confront and forgive one another on a regular basis. The form tutor has the potential to develop the group through experience, reflection and the celebration of what has happened. In this way life experience becomes their teacher, and the whole group learns together. The chaplain can help to uncover, in the work of the form tutor, some of the deeper reasons for hoping and believing in the goodness of all the pupils in their care. The chaplain's role is not to tell the tutors how to do their job, but to help them find the vocational roots of their role, so that working as a form tutor will feed their own spirit in a way that helps them to persevere with their sacred task.

Prayer and pastoral systems

The chaplain can help to weave a school community together by the way prayer is used to support pastoral concerns. In a Christian community, the instinctive response to needs is the prayer of intercession. This is a faith response that needs a visible expression in school. Form tutors may ask pupils to pray for needs in class, and assembly prayers often include prayers of intercessions. Apart from these formal moments, the chaplain, in response to conversations, can offer to pray for others' intentions. Small prayer groups in school can adopt these intentions as part of their pattern of prayer. The chaplain may also want to do an occasional silent prayer collection by handing out slips of paper and asking pupils to write an intention or a symbol to express their prayer for another member of the school community and those can be taken to a school Eucharist. The provision of prayer boxes in each pastoral office and some slips of paper nearby can allow pastoral staff to suggest to certain pupils that a prayer for another person, for themselves or for peace at home might be a way to end a difficult conversation. The safety of such prayer slips and their collection should lie with the chaplain, who can ensure their confidentiality and link them to the prayer of the Church. The development of circles of prayer, in feeder parishes, can help to make further links to the wider Church and especially when these can be maintained through a good website for prayer and an occasional prayer meeting based at school. The ability of prayer to be used in a variety of ways, across a school community, means that it can help engage spiritually with the pastoral needs of the school and become a visible sign of the spirit that animates the whole school.

Conclusion

Pastoral care in a Christian school is not simply the removal of obstacles to teaching and learning. Pastoral care is a response to every child as a whole person with specific needs, a unique story and a sacred dignity. Don Bosco recognised young people as the most precious and yet most vulnerable part of society. Most adults working in school are also moved to respond to the precious potential and frailty of each young person. The chaplain's role is to help sustain the motivation of the adults by opening up deeper reasons for the hard work and self-sacrifice that many adults bring to this pastoral role.

Chapter Five
Ministry & Chaplaincy

> This is what is needed: a Church for young people, which will know how to speak to their heart and enkindle, comfort, and inspire enthusiasm in it with the joy of the Gospel and the strength of the Eucharist; a Church which will know how to invite and welcome the person who seeks a purpose for which to commit his whole existence; a Church which is not afraid to require much, after having given much; which does not fear asking from young people the effort of a noble and authentic adventure, such as that of the following of the Gospel.[24]

It was stated, at the outset, that Chaplaincy was an informal ministry that is conducted within a formal school setting. The majority of recipients of this informal ministry are young people. However this informal ministry is aimed at the whole community and not simply the young. It is a multi-generational ministry that needs to reach the youngest arrival and the oldest member of the community on the verge of retirement. One of the most useful models for understanding the informal dimension of chaplaincy is provided by the Catholic Bishops of the USA. Their model of youth ministry provides a comprehensive framework, within which the varied work of chaplaincy can find a pastoral shape rationale. The full text of the *Vision of Catholic Youth Ministry* can be found by following the reference below or bought through any bookseller.[25] This book, celebrating thirty years of this approach to youth ministry, outlines a number of components some of which will be in the next two chapters. First of all, it is worth noting that this comprehensive framework begins by outlining three goals for youth ministry which can be applied to the whole-school community:

- To empower the school community to live as disciples of Jesus Christ in the world today.

- To draw the school community into responsible participation in the life, mission and work of the Church.

- To foster the total personal and spiritual growth of each person in the school community.

The goals focus on drawing people as individuals and groups into a personal experience of Gospel living and a relationship to Christ. It involves exploring gifts and choices and creating the confidence for individuals to make a difference to their world. For the chaplain the youth focus of these goals must extend, where

---

[24] Pope John Paul II. 1995 World Day of Prayer for Vocations.
[25] St Mary's Press, U.S. (Jul 2005) http://www.usccb.org/laity/youth/rtvcontents.shtml

appropriate, to working with the staff, where many of the same needs and opportunities exist in a different context. For those who are supervising and evaluating chaplaincy in school, these three goals, and the components that follow, can form a useful background against which to assess the breadth and effectiveness of chaplaincy provision. A format for such evaluation has been suggested in chapter seven of this handbook.

The components that follow are described individually but the whole approach is comprehensive. No one component stands alone but is a focal point that merges into the others. The justice component for example leads to an engagement with issues that develop the leadership component. The liturgy and worship component emerges from the community building component which in turn may lead back to leadership and pastoral care. The components below are presented in no specific order and are reflected upon in the context of a school chaplaincy.

Building community

The task of ministering lies with the whole-school community and not solely with the chaplaincy. In a Christian community, no one is exempt from behaviours that build belonging, participation, safety, celebration and healing. The first ministers to young people in the school are other young people. The adults in the school are called upon to create a safe environment in which young people can grow in self-confidence and spiritual awareness. The chaplain, through example and knowledge, creates a space where belonging, celebration and compassion can break down barriers of mistrust and allow hearts to be opened. This co-responsibility for one another in the school community is an expression of the inner life of God, as a trinity in which the giving and receiving of loving kindness becomes the energy behind all of creation. That self-sacrificing and honest care for others, within and beyond the school community, is an act of faith in life that is ultimately more important than any creed that will ever be written.

Chaplaincy has a particular responsibility in establishing and nurturing life-giving networks of loving kindness in school. This can happen simply by introducing one needy person to another who can offer support that may grow into friendship. Community can be built by matching personal needs and gifts in a myriad of patterns from sports to social enterprise and from pantomimes to planning meetings. The formation of small groups that never become cliques is a strategy and a skill that is central to chaplaincy provision. A chaplaincy is a focal point for a wide range of groups, touching different levels of school life: A justice group can form for short or long periods and operate in a single year group or across the whole school. Liturgy and prayer groups reach out to a specific need in some young people. Practical service groups engage gifts and encourage leadership in other young people. Support groups focus on specific needs in the school and build the sense of compassion across the school community. Some groups consciously mix ages and include staff members in order to build the whole-school sense of community.

Schools have a statutory duty to promote community cohesion and the work of the chaplaincy can be a very helpful contribution to this area of school development. The document issued by the Catholic Education Service, on promoting cohesion, makes it clear that community cohesion is neither new nor an option for Catholic schools.[26] All Catholic schools welcome people of other faiths wherever spaces are available. Every person is born, grows and develops within relationships and that bond is part of the mystery of who we are as people. The individualism promoted by our present culture can only be overcome by deepening the spiritual bonds that hold people together. Working in groups, experiencing variety and celebrating diversity are spiritual expressions of a common humanity. Catholic schools have a good record in welcoming diversity, recognising the needs of individual groups and building links between them and then extending those links into the local community. The chaplaincy is not a service for a select few, but is an integrating element in a school that reaches out in Gospel faith to the local community and to the wider world.

These groups may not be the direct responsibility of the chaplain but the chaplain would be expected to be aware of them, involved from time to time and able to encourage and support the pupils and staff who make them happen. For the chaplain, the clusters of people, on corridors and the gatherings in staffroom, are all sacred spaces. The chaplain is called to see the words of Jesus coming true at every moment in the school community, *whenever two or three are gathered in my name, there I am in the middle of them.*[27] Becoming aware of this sacred presence, revealed in human relationships, is central to the chaplain's work. To reflect on God within the ordinary events of life, helping the busy school community to be aware of God's presence, is one of the ways that the chaplain safeguards the spiritual treasures of the school. That spiritual treasure gives individuals the energy to persevere in kindness, to have the courage to admit mistakes and the generosity to celebrate the success of others in the school. It is an energy that sustains the community in difficult times, preserves individual dignity and creates a safe place for personal gifts to grow to maturity.

---

[26] Catholic Education Service *Catholic Schools and Community Cohesion* February 2008
[27] Mt 18:19

Evangelisation

Evangelisation means announcing the good news of the Gospel through action and in words. It means *doing the Gospel* and not just talking about it. The chaplain, in a school community, will be looked to as a model of Gospel living and as an inspiration for others to do the same. Like most ministers, whether they are priests or lay people, the chaplain carries the burden of trying to live authentic Gospel ideals in a public setting. When dealing with groups and individuals, the chaplain will be scrutinised by those who are seeking a role-model of Christian living. The main relationship of the chaplain with people is not to command and control, nor is the chaplain committed to deliver a curriculum. Instead, the chaplain is required to be the good news for the individual or the group with whom they are working. The Gospel is the chaplain's curriculum delivered through whatever tasks, needs and dreams that people present each day.

Unlike the teacher, who approaches specific groups at fixed times, with a clear curriculum based task, the chaplain works by invitation, offering a response to the perceived needs of individuals and groups in the school. This is because true evangelisation can only happen when it is freely chosen by those involved. In the Gospels, Jesus used this same invitational approach with his disciples and allowed them the freedom to refuse. Evangelisation is always an offer that is made persuasively but without pressure. It is never domineering or manipulative. Instead it is a free choice that is offered, in season and out of season, by the chaplain to those who wish to engage. Therefore a chaplain needs to have a steady flow of small invitations ready to draw people into engagement with the Gospel on their own terms.

Evangelisation checklist

This is a short list of evangelisation tasks for all adults who work in school but it applies especially to chaplains and headteachers.

1 Less words - More action

Preach the Gospel always, if necessary use words is wise advice, attributed to St Francis of Assisi. Authentic witness to the Gospel has to be active so that the words and behaviour of a chaplain reinforce each other. Therefore a friendly approach, a quiet word in the ear, a cheerful manner, plenty of praise and the courage to stop damaging behaviour are a visible witness to young people of deeper Gospel values.

2 Take risks

Move into groups and situations where you do not always feel at ease and where you may not be in control of events. Move conversations into areas of interest for the other person. Be in the world of the adolescent and staff members, without becoming aligned and build an awareness of their hopes and fears.

3 Recognising the moment

Extended contact with groups and individuals builds a familiarity with their values and interests as well as with the pattern of relationships and individual histories involved. This background knowledge and experience will help the chaplain to recognise the moment when it is appropriate to move the conversation to a deeper level of awareness, without manipulating or smuggling religion into the setting. Recognising the links between the Gospel, sacraments and the daily life of individuals can build bridges of understanding between the formal aspects of religion and the experience of an inner spiritual life.

4 Proclaim the Gospel

This is the part that most people recognise as evangelisation: the reading, celebration and reflection on the Gospel in formal settings of prayer and the sacraments. It is a vital part of the process, but only a part. There is a need for a clear presentation of the person of Jesus and the story of his life, death and resurrection. For adolescents, this proclamation needs to be far more than an abstract presentation of a philosophy of life. It has to be an offer of an inner relationship with Christ, clothed in living experience and tailored to the concerns of young people's lives and work. That means that chaplains have to consciously model Gospel values in all their activities. Other staff members should be encouraged to recognise that their way of working with the young can be an expression of Gospel values. The opportunity for staff to speak about their life and faith can be helpful for many others in the school community and the chaplain can consciously create occasions for this to happen.

5 Transforming action

Proclaiming the Gospel is not the last word in evangelisation. The last word is always transformation. The most important transformations in the Christian story are always hidden; the resurrection happened quietly in the dead of night, the nativity was hidden in an obscure stable of an inn. In a similar way, the transformations of faith are rarely visible to the chaplain but buried in the obscurity of young hearts and minds that may be oblivious to that deep change in their search for meaning.

Another kind of transforming action is one that confirms the ability of young people and adults in the school to make a difference to their world. The engagement with gifts that evoke a call to action is part of the process of saying a **Yes** to the Gospel in activity if not in words. In doing so, those who take action begin to live the Gospel dream and become disciples on a journey that builds hope and meaning in other's lives. They begin to be good news for others, without an imposed piety or any excessive God-talk.

Justice and Service

When Jesus began his public work he announced his mission by using the words of the prophet Isaiah:

> **To bring good news to the poor, freedom to captives, sight for the blind. (Luke 4:18-19)**

Right from the start of his ministry, Jesus saw his work as one of liberating people from poverty, sickness and captivity. In a school community that is trying to live the Gospel, this dimension of practical service should have a major role. The social teaching of the Church is an under-used resource for schools who want to develop the justice and service component of the chaplaincy. CAFOD has reminded us of one piece of social teaching through the *live simply* campaign by highlighting the fortieth anniversary of Pope Paul VI document on the progress of people, listed in the resources as *Populorum Progressio*.[28] The link between Gospel and life will often expose injustice, help to identify vulnerable groups and awaken the call to service. One of the tasks of chaplaincy is to ensure that the Gospel is not marginalised but used to build right relationships and, where necessary, challenge current school practice.

---

[28] Full text is available at: http://www.osjspm.org/majordoc_populorum_progressio_official_text.aspx

A right relationship to other groups and individuals means recognising three important aspects of human life:

Frailty
Despite all our technology and power, humanity is frail and fleeting. We are all easy prey to deprivation, addictions and violence and we cannot stand apart from it and say it has nothing to do with me.

Freedom
Despite our individual frailty, we are also unique and called to freedom, to make choices, to take risks and to create our own unique sacred journey.

Solidarity
We need each other to grow into fullness of life, to manage our frailty and find our freedom. We cannot be human on our own and we find fullness of meaning only in relationship to others.

The Gospel is a charter for right relationships that uncovers these three areas of human experience, naming the mystery behind all human life as a Father who cares for his children. Wherever frailty, freedom and solidarity emerge as issues in the school or the wider community the Gospel becomes a map for a journey into right relationships. Proclaiming the Gospel in good times and bad is the task of the school community under the guidance of the headteacher and the chaplain.

A second theme, in the justice and service area, is the balancing of rights and responsibilities. Again, this theme works at a personal level and at the level of a wider community. Those who have the least voice, those most vulnerable and those at risk should become a focus of responsibility for others in school. In supporting that needy group the school learns how to be compassionate, and non-judgmental. The school becomes a generous and a just community. The chaplain, therefore, has a role to encourage service groups and focus them on specific needs, within and around the school community. How does a chaplain identify which projects are appropriate and which should be supported? Here are some questions that can help to clarify the priorities in choosing justice and service projects within a school community.

Choosing appropriate justice and service projects
- Where are the focal points of enthusiasm among staff and pupils? What issues and areas of the world and the locality are prominent in their awareness?

- What particular gifts, strengths and traditions does the school community have that might suggest a match with the deprivations and frailties of others, locally and globally?

- What national and local campaigns are operating currently that fit the concerns and the gifts of the school community?

- How many long-term and short-term projects can the school community sustain and how can they be paced through an academic year?

- What is the balance between justice and service in the projects the school has already adopted?

- How committed is the school community to justice and service? How are justice and service recognised and promoted, across the whole school?

- What particular gifts, enthusiasms and experience can the chaplain bring to issues of justice and service?

- How do we keep a clear balance between fundraising and awareness-raising, between service to others and campaigning on issues?

With such questions and others, a chaplain can begin to integrate the justice and service projects into the overall planning of the school community. In addressing these needs, the chaplain is offering an effective invitation into a relationship with Jesus, who came to set people free. The option to work hard for others is an invitation therefore to continue a personal and community faith journey toward the justice and peace of God's kingdom.

Leader development

One of the greatest gifts that chaplaincy can offer to the school community, and to the world, is providing reflective and committed leaders for the future. Work on this aspect of chaplaincy is a hidden investment in the future. It may not be measurable or even visible during the school life of pupils or staff but the experience of supporting others, working together and taking the initiative, lays down foundations for building honest citizens and good Christians for the decades that lie ahead.

The second goal of informal ministry, mentioned at the start of this chapter, is to draw young people and adults into responsible participation in the life and mission of the local faith community. The chaplain in a school is well placed to identify and create opportunities for such responsible participation that can help many people refine their leadership skills, in a caring and learning environment. There are many places in the school curriculum where such leadership opportunities already flourish: in peer-mentoring programmes, prefect systems, award and service schemes as well as the consultative and democratic roles of class representatives and school councils. Staff too, have the opportunity to grow in leadership by volunteering to lead small groups, engaging with specific issues, accessing training and representing each other's needs and concerns, within the school community. In a similar way, identifying these experiences as vocational moments allows the chaplain to assist in deepening the experience so that, in working for each other, people are able to discover their giftedness and explore the spiritual call to action that peer working always evokes.

Chaplaincy needs to ensure that there is an appropriate training and accreditation pattern working through informal groups. Such training may highlight and celebrate the discovery of new gifts and skills in young people. Recognition of growth in this area has been organised by CAFOD through the *liveit!* campaign allowing personal growth to be linked with the spirit of the Gospel and a specific Church agency.[29] In a similar way, Young Catholic Workers (YCW) provides training, networking and accreditation through the *Impact* programme.[30] Training builds confidence, aids reflection and helps with vocational discernment. The chaplain has to ensure that training for leadership also has a spiritual and reflective dimension, so that the mystery and wonder of emerging skills might be traced back into deeper motives and the dignity of individual young people. A chaplain can make a contribution to training by encouraging retreats, affirming conversations with potential leaders and offering simple discernment experiences to draw out the depth of the experience of emerging leaders and its vocational significance.

Catechesis

Youth and school ministry has always included a dimension of catechesis. Even after all the sacramental programmes are completed, catechesis continues as a life-long process. The Universal Catechism of The Catholic Church describes catechesis as including the following:

• The initial proclamation of the Gospel to arouse faith.

---

[29] http://bigdeal.cafod.org.uk/action/liveit/leader2
[30] http://www.ycwimpact.com

- The examination of reasons for belief.

- The experience of Christian living.

- The celebration of the sacraments.

- Integration into the ecclesial community.

- Apostolic witness.[31]

John Paul II described the purpose of catechesis in this way,

> **The definitive aim of catechesis is to put people not only in touch, but in communion, in intimacy, with Jesus Christ.**[32]

In the light of such a definition, it is clear that every teacher in a Catholic school shares some part of the task of catechesis. Every teacher in a Catholic school is committed to working within an ethos that has the Gospel and the person of Jesus at the centre of all it does. The way that a teacher approaches relationships with pupils, manages discipline, celebrates success and shares their own weakness, will proclaim or contradict the message of the Gospel built into the mission statement of their school. One of the chaplain's tasks is to help teachers make connections between their own good practice and its deeper roots in the Gospel. Praising a young person will make good educational sense and help motivate a pupil to work better. Recognising that such praise also celebrates and respects the dignity and mystery of that pupil, opens up that same event as a lived proclamation of the Gospel in action. Recognising the spiritual dimension in good teaching opens up spiritual energy for teachers, which will help them persevere in their vocation and find the motivation to persevere.

James Gallagher identifies three aspects of catechesis as it appears in a school setting:

- The general ethos, climate or atmosphere of the school as it is inspired by the Christian vision of faith.

- The voluntary catechetical activities which should take place in school.

- The teaching of religion as a classroom subject.[33]

---

[31] The Universal Catechism of The Catholic Church No 6
[32] John Paul II Catechesis in our time No 5
[33] James Gallagher SDB Soil for The Seed p298

The paschal mystery, the Easter story, is being lived out in every life in every school every day. The chaplain's work should help that reality emerge and be named and celebrated clearly in school every day. The tradition of the Church offers Gospel stories that find echoes in the daily experience of school life, creating opportunities for catechesis in many conversations every day. In the saints, whose feasts are celebrated in the liturgical year, the Church provides models for living and more opportunities for catechesis. Drawing a school together into well planned celebrations of liturgy and sacraments provides a further whole-school setting for catechesis. Finally, the school community finds opportunities to witness to the Gospel, by involvement in the needs of the local community and sharing the life of the local church that will support the adult faith of the pupils into the future.

The second aspect of catechesis, identified by James Gallagher, takes place in the formation of voluntary groups, especially where the spiritual dimension is more explicit. The voluntary nature of the group means that there is a freedom of choice being exercised that is central to the catechetical relationship. The catechesis happens not only in the action taken but also in the reflection on the experience of serving others. In reflection on the compassion, self-sacrifice and the uncertainty of serving others, a young person is already in touch with the person of Jesus, if they could but name it. The adult, working reflectively with a group, can help those connections to be made by the young people at their own pace and in their own language. The same staff member getting involved in a staff retreat day is taking responsibility for their own ongoing formation as a Christian and is as much the focus of the chaplain's role as the young people.

The spiritual focus becomes more explicit in groups that are formed around the tasks of prayer and liturgy. These groups need more specific spiritual formation and skills, if they are to achieve their aims. Building prayer and silence into such groups can be very helpful in nurturing an atmosphere of listening and a sense of the sacred in what is being done. In prayer groups, the sense of the sacred is central to the group task. In this kind of group, be it a lively group using music or a more contemplative group exploring silence, the potential for spiritual growth and catechesis is at its greatest.

These groups are part of the normal life of a Catholic school, but it is not the chaplain's job to run them all. The chaplain's role is to monitor the potential for such groups, in partnership with other adult staff and initiate as many as can be sustained for different age groups.

The final aspect of catechesis in school, mentioned by James Gallagher, takes place in the context of Religious Education, within the formal classroom setting. A sustained examination of the content and reasons for belief is part of the catechetical task. The aim of religious education is to develop people who can think spiritually, ethically and theologically as well as being aware of the content of Christian faith and other world religions. Unlike some other academic areas, Religious Education can become holistic in its impact in every lesson. Questions of meaning, morals, life and death are part of the core of its curriculum that tend to flow outwards into the personal world of pupils, raising issues that are vital and yet unanswerable within the constraints of the curriculum content. The school needs to recognise the spiritual theme that will emerge in every lesson and might find the OFSTED document on the evaluation of the spiritual, moral and social dimensions of learning helpful, in focussing this core theme across the curriculum. The full document is referenced below.[34]

Part of the dilemma of the Religious Education teacher, faced with wide spiritual potential raised in the classroom, can be resolved by good chaplaincy provision. The chaplain has a specific role in supporting and working in partnership with Religious Education staff. In particular, the chaplain can provide the opportunity for a range of extension activities that can link directly with the Religious Education curriculum. Planning around the curriculum, together with the department, allows the chaplain to identify opportunities to extend the catechetical dimension of Religious Education teaching. For example, a section of work on the social teaching of the Church could become the context for recruiting a small group to do some direct activity for the poor or needy. The group may be short-lived but their experience, and reflection upon it, could be fed back into the classroom at a later date.

Advocacy

One of the core components of youth ministry is described as advocacy. The literal meaning of the word involves being called to stand by another person. In common usage, advocacy also means speaking for and on behalf of another person or group in a public forum, where for some reason their voice may not be heard. Advocacy describes a relationship in which one person identifies the needs of another and with their permission, tries to make those needs known in the wider community.

---

[34] http://www.ofsted.gov.uk/assets/3598.doc

The theology behind advocacy rests upon the understanding that a community, seeking guidance from the Holy Spirit, needs to be able to hear the lived experience of the whole community, if it is to make balanced Gospel-centred choices. The Gospel is full of stories where it is the marginal voice that often grasps reality most clearly: the grateful leper, the prodigal son and Zacheus all saw things differently from the edge of established groups. The chaplain, seeking to follow the Gospel, needs to ensure that marginal voices are heard, if the signs of the time are to be read clearly in school. The context of advocacy is therefore a kind of *spiritual democracy* in which every voice has a right and a duty to be heard in the community. This does not imply a crude voting system for every major decision but rather that every voice has been heard and valued appropriately in the complexity of the decision-making processes in school.

A school chaplain has a specific role in the community that involves listening with empathy to a wide range of views. Many of these issues will be confidential and not be appropriate to share in the public forum. Other issues will have a natural place in the planning and decision-making processes of the school. The chaplain who wishes to become an advocate for others must be prepared to reflect on experience and speak on behalf of voices that may never be heard in the classroom, in the playground, or in the staff room.

Advocacy operates most clearly and often urgently when rights and responsibilities are out of balance in a school community. The United Nations Convention on the Rights of the Child (UNCRC)[35] outlines some basic rights that may require advocacy from time to time in school. According to that Convention, children have, amongst others, the following rights:

- To express their views. (12)

- To information. (13)

- To form their own groups. (15)

- To privacy. (16)

- To a clean environment. (24)

- To protection from harm. (32)

---

[35] See www.unicef.org.uk, the numbers in the list refer to sections of the convention.

As children grow into young adults, the importance of some of these rights increases if they are to grow in self-esteem and self-determination. It is easy in a busy school, with complex choices, to underestimate the importance of young people exercising these rights within the community. The convention also outlines the corresponding responsibilities that young people must adopt if their rights generally are to be maintained: They include the responsibility to respect others, to learn to the best of their ability, to protect the environment and those most at risk, including those with different beliefs and cultures. In ministering to young people, as an advocate, the chaplain will be challenged to help balance the rights and responsibilities of many people in the school community and to root those rights and responsibilities firmly into a Gospel-based ethos. A fuller treatment of this chapter will be available at www.salesians.org.uk/chap.

Chapter Six
Ministry & Chaplaincy (2)

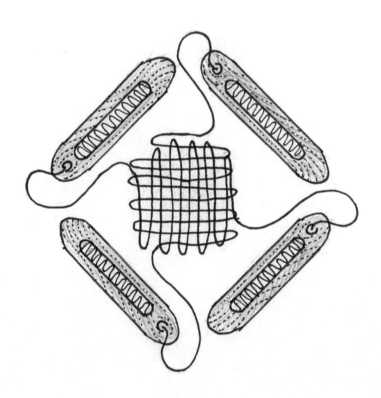

Pastoral Care

Pastoral care lies close to the heart of all ministry and chaplaincy. The Vision of Catholic Youth Ministry identifies four aspects of pastoral care for the young which apply to the whole-school community:

- Caring deeply for the young.

- Confronting them honestly.

- Meeting them where they are.

- Showing a way to wholeness of life.

This pattern of active and sometimes preventive compassion is rooted in the image of Jesus as the Good Shepherd presented in the tenth chapter of St John's Gospel. In that description seven aspects, seem to offer a scriptural perspective on the pastoral role of the chaplain:

- Knowing the sheep individually and celebrating their growth.

- Having a detailed knowledge of the country.

- Vigilant in watching for wolves and other threats.

- Creating sheepfolds, safe places for the sheep.

- Laying down his life when needed.

- Open to other sheep joining the flock.

- Constantly moving to new pasture.

These seven areas of the shepherding experience will be used to reflect on the pastoral role of the chaplain in school. The identification of the chaplain with the good shepherd is not exclusive but one that all those who work with the young and the vulnerable will share, to some extent. It is also a role that involves a balanced and optimistic approach that avoids the model of the *trauma chaplain* who only appears when things have gone wrong. The same list could be used to reflect on the work of counsellors, teachers, health workers and parents. It is a pastoral model for all carers. These elements of shepherding offer particular challenges to those involved in sixth form colleges where students arrive from a variety of background and varying degrees of established peer support. In these settings hospitality and awareness need to be established quickly in a college life that may only last for just two years. Similar challenges exist for chaplains who are involved in the transition from primary into secondary education. The chaplain may not have much time to give at such transition moments but can try to recognise and support those who do that work in school. Reflecting on some of the qualities listed below may also stimulate reflection and the creativity of the school in directing the work of the chaplain at these times.

Knowing and celebrating the sheep by name

Much of the chaplain's work is built upon the ability to establish friendly relationships with a wide variety of individuals and groups, across the school community. This ability is presented as a core skill in most job descriptions since chaplaincy is a relational ministry and not simply a set of functional tasks and targets. The ability to express loving kindness, availability, celebration, warmth and moral strength helps the chaplain to engage positively with large numbers in the school. Knowing and remembering a lot of individuals is an important gift for the chaplain. At the heart of this friendly, personal and respectful approach, is an act of faith that God is being encountered in the friendly relationship. The chaplain builds this friendly approach on the basis of his or her own personality, as different groups and individuals are drawn to them. The chaplain is also challenged to move beyond their own natural attraction to particular personalities, to engage in a friendly approach with others who are different and less comfortable to be with.

Being able to move beyond one's natural inclinations in forming friendly links is vital in avoiding the creation of cliques, where the chaplaincy becomes a club for like-minded people, who happen to get on with the chaplain. Being able to sustain relationships across the school community ensures that the chaplaincy is a whole-school ministry and not a solo act on the stage of school life. This last point is one of the stronger arguments for a team-based approach to chaplaincy. The wise chaplain will, therefore, intentionally cultivate friendly links with young people and adults, who are significantly different in personality, so that the impact of chaplaincy can move into a wider circle of needs and skills and make the chaplain more available to the whole-school community.

Knowing the country

The shepherd, of St John's Gospel, knows the land he walks and the resources and dangers that it holds. Each school site is unique in its resources and its dangers; it takes time to explore and to know thoroughly. A school has a geography that gives up its secrets to the adult observer, bit by bit. It begins by knowing where classrooms and offices are, but quickly moves into more subtle perceptions. Knowing the geography of a school implies knowing how the pupils see the school, the names they use for certain areas and the way they populate the school, especially at break times. For some pupils there may be territorial spaces for different year groups, dangerous spaces and safe places that, to an adult, look exactly the same. It is instructive for the chaplain, on occasion, to ask pupils to walk the school with them and tell them what areas they like, which they avoid, what names and memories are linked to certain places and what level of comfort they feel. Knowing those things will help the chaplain learn about the pastoral care that may be needed and where to spend time when walking the school, especially at recreation times. The same sense of mood and territory will apply in a staffroom as much as in the school yard; there will be no-go areas, self-contained huddles and a general mood attached to staffrooms and offices that will, perhaps unconsciously, block some and welcome others. Once again, the chaplain's pastoral care should lead them to establish a friendly presence in spaces even if they feel, at times, uncomfortable and unwelcomed. The presence of the chaplain can often help to create a more positive atmosphere in the places visited and break down the hidden boundaries that exclude others in the school community.

The other dimension to knowing the country for the chaplain goes beyond geography to the landscape of adolescence. This changing landscape lies in the experience of each young person as they grow from childhood to being adults. The chaplain, reading that landscape will recognise the changing patterns of friendship, the young person's sense of their own body and the turbulence of their emotional life. The growing sense of independence, integrity and the increase in the capacity for critical thinking mark out adolescence as a special terrain that leaves the young person rich in opportunity but vulnerable to exploitation. The chaplain, walking the world of adolescence needs to encourage the opportunities and guard against exploitation. In that landscape the chaplain can also expect to have cherished beliefs attacked unreasonably and important issues met with boredom. Staying with adolescents in the peaks and troughs of joy and despair is part of the pastoral care the chaplain can offer. Helping colleagues and young people to support their peers in this way is time well spent for the chaplain since it expands the skills and the impact of pastoral care across the whole community.

Being vigilant

Pastoral care is not simply about responding to requests for support but also about anticipating needs and dangers, before they become explicit. Chaplains, with lively imaginations, will learn to predict what might happen in the future and what pastoral needs and opportunities might occur. Noticing, for example, that prefects are being over zealous in use of their authority with younger pupils may lead the chaplain to share their concern with the staff member about training. Similarly, hearing some resentment expressed in the staffroom might lead to a quiet conversation that breaks no confidences with a member of the school-leadership group. Noticing small things and acting to calm, educate or alert others is part of pastoral care for all staff. For the chaplain, it is a special duty because of their privileged overview of the school and their duty to safeguard the spiritual values at the heart of a school.

Vigilance does not only apply to the identification of dangers but also to recognising opportunity. The potential of an event such as the launch of Philip Pullman's *Golden Compass* film created a pastoral opportunity for reflection as a school community on spirituality and young people. The arrival of the Olympics in London during 2012 creates other possibilities. These predictable events can be drawn into the pastoral-care plan of the school, when they are anticipated well in advance. Other smaller events can be recognised as pastoral opportunities, even the delay of a school bus might lead to the opportunity for a small group to share a discussion, do some work or get to know each other better at the school bus-stop.

Vigilance about the impact of tried-and-tested events in the school calendar is an important part of the pastoral dimension of the school. Some events are entered automatically into the school calendar, long after they have outlived their usefulness and purpose in the school plan. It is an act of pastoral care for the school to recognise events that have become more of a burden than a blessing on the school year. Vigilance and critical thinking, in this area, can lift many burdens from staff, pupils and parents. The renewal of these events or their ending is part of liberation from habits that no longer serve the spirit of the school. The danger however is that such events are taken away and not replaced so that the overall pastoral energy of the school declines and less events take place.

Creating sheepfolds

A chaplain has a special duty to be aware of those who are most at risk, in the school community. It is a role in school that is shared by every adult but the chaplain is called upon to make the spiritual roots of this role transparent in chaplaincy work. The chaplaincy can be seen as a kind of sheepfold; a special place in the school where physical and psychological security is central to all that happens. In the chaplaincy, the dimensions of every caring school-relationship should become visible to the rest of the school. Warmth, welcome, guidance, compassion, respect, understanding, affection, humour and celebration should become tangible experiences in the chaplaincy base and become a symbol of what each educative relationship in school strives towards. It should be a sign and a bearer of God's love to the young and for the whole school.

There is a sense in which the quality of listening, the appropriate use of confidentiality and a non-judgmental approach create a personal safe space for everyone in the school community. Every teacher carries a responsibility to become a safe place for young people and the chaplaincy should be a support and a model for that safety. The fact that a young person can come to a chaplaincy and be quiet and talk when they are ready is a symbol of their unique experience of God's presence at work in their lives. Staff, too, will use the space offered by chaplaincy, especially when the stresses and strains of work and living become difficult to contain. Often the chaplain needs to simply create the space and leave people free to recover, rest and think. In most cases, the chaplain can assist individuals by creating the space within which people are capable of resolving their own dilemmas.

Laying down one's life

Self-sacrifice seems to be an expected element in a chaplain's job description. Pastoral care takes on its most effective form when it works beyond the expected limits and goes that extra mile in meeting other's needs. The note to a staff member on the anniversary of a bereavement, because it goes beyond the expected, has an unexpected impact for good. Staying late in school to meet parents or prepare a group for confirmation, after a long confusing day, is not to be expected. Such voluntary activity represents self-sacrifice for the chaplain and also for those who will have to deal with their absence at home. All those involved in education are drawn inexorably into self-sacrifice and into going that extra mile. Teaching and chaplaincy have a vocational dimension that means the work is relational and establishes bonds that go beyond the simple bullet points of a printed job description.

The chaplain, however, is particularly vulnerable, along with other teaching staff, to self-neglect rather than self-sacrifice, in their serving of the young. The chaplain may come to see the extra mile as being expected by the school and not as a personal gift they can give to the school community. When that happens then resentment is not far behind. If the situation continues, burnout will inevitably follow. Part of the discipline of chaplaincy is to establish a balance between the needs of the school and the long-term capacity of the chaplain to meet those needs. Acceptance of one's own physical and psychological limitations is a key skill for the chaplain. Matching personal gifts and energy to the needs presented by the school should be the basis for a detailed job-description that should be monitored in the regular supervision that is essential for this role in school. Managing the expectations of the school about the potential of an individual chaplain is part of the task of their line-manager so that a job description emerges that is clear and realistic. Where the chaplain chooses to go the extra mile they must be free to do so. The school, guided by the line-manager, should not slip into unrealistic expectations from their chaplain that may lead to long-term psychological and physical damage. However, a wise line-manager should also invite the chaplain to consider whose needs are being met, through some of their work. It is all too easy to start to meet one's own needs and pursue one's own enthusiasms, through the young people. *Laying down one's life* means putting oneself at the service of the young, as their needs change and develop.

Openness to other sheep

The chaplain is called to form and work with groups that are life-giving to the whole-school community. Having a range of different groups available for pupils and staff expands the opportunity for a wide range of contact-making chaplaincy, a relational ministry that can reach every part of the school. Each group will have its own dynamic and will progress through stages where it will need to consolidate itself before it moves into work for others. One of the dangers of such small groups is the tendency to become exclusive and overly concerned with their own needs rather than the needs of the wider community. Whilst all groups will have a therapeutic dimension, chaplaincy groups need to have a purposeful focus on the needs of others, if they are to be authentic experiences of Gospel and Church. The chaplain needs to keep looking at these groups, and beyond these groups, to see who is being included and who is being excluded, in the work of the chaplaincy.

Identifying which groups are open and ready for new membership is an art that links the chaplain to the Good Shepherd. Grouping individuals in ways that lead them to thrive is an art that depends upon knowing the strong and the weak and helping them to help each other. The chaplain has to have a particular eye for the outcast, the loner and the marginal, in the playground and in the staffroom. Recognising them and offering invitations to involvement and being available means that the chaplaincy will never become a place for a cosy clique, but rather a place where needs and gifts meet in an ever-changing pattern of loving kindness. Again this aspect of chaplaincy is merely a visible modelling of what most teaching staff will achieve in the classroom each day in the placing of pupils in the classroom and the constant encouragement to support one another in their learning.

Constantly moving on

The task of the shepherd is to bring the sheep to best pasture, to keep them safe and keep them together. All these things imply that a shepherd has to adapt and move according to the seasons and the threats that come and go each day. Being a shepherd involves a semi-nomadic existence and so does chaplaincy. The core task of chaplaincy is to respond to the spiritual needs of the school community. The chaplaincy is not concerned to set up a fixed service into which the needs of pupils must fit themselves. Instead the chaplaincy is a flexible response to the changing needs of the school, its local area and the specific needs of the students.

In chaplaincy, as in all youth ministry, there is a need to be always starting again. The needs and the environment are always changing and that will demand adaptation from the chaplain. But the need for change in chaplaincy and youth ministry is based on a more fundamental aspect of the work - for each young person the world is new, the skills they are discovering are new and they want to make a creative and personal impact on their world. They do not want so much to inherit the past but to create the future. Therefore, young people prefer to start afresh and make their own mark. So chaplaincy needs to be starting again, always provisional and never fixed and final. For that reason chaplaincy will not have the same predictability of patterning in school life that department and curriculum areas are able to achieve. The tendency of chaplaincy to work flexibly and change direction, as young people's contribution changes, is part of its strength and also part of the frustration in integrating it effectively into school planning. Just when a chaplaincy project seems settled, well integrated into the pattern of school life, it can change direction or disappear altogether. Whilst some core activities around liturgy, pastoral care and leadership will always be present, how those areas are addressed can change significantly, as young people make their impact on planning, and take some ownership of the tasks. The chaplain must live with the tension between meeting the needs of the whole school and providing realistic experiences of youth-group involvement in responding to those needs.

Prayer and Worship

Prayer is a response to the mystery of God. It involves the whole person - mind, body, feelings, memories, relationships, inspirations and dreams. We search this mysterious presence for answers, for practical help, for meaning and for guidance in life. We pray in thanksgiving, we petition God and ask for forgiveness. In a religious setting, we use common patterns of prayer, sacred symbols and sacraments that reach back into a collective memory and bring that continuous presence of God into a sharper focus, in a worshipping community.

For the chaplain, this area of human experience is a core concern. It is in some ways the source and the summit of the chaplain's role in school and college. Each person, in the school community, brings their own unique pattern of spiritual experience. For some, that experience is sharp and clear and expressed in specific religious language. For most, the spiritual experience they carry is submerged and vague and not easily accessed or expressed personally, let alone in a public setting. For some young people, the idea of expressing this aspect of their experience can be profoundly embarrassing, perhaps too precious to them for it to be caught up in traditional faith language. For other young people, even the existence of an inner spiritual life may come as something of a surprise since they do not consciously reflect on their own thoughts and feelings but live in a very practical *what you see is what you get* world. They are left skimming on the surface of life, without any apparent depth of spirit. Staff too, have a variety of needs in this area, which a chaplain can address by good relationships and well planned spiritual experiences. Sometimes the best thing a chaplain can do for the young people in the school is to support and energise the motives of their teachers.

This vast range of readiness for prayer and worship poses the chaplain some very difficult challenges: How can a community express a common ethos and spirit when so many are at different stages of awareness? How can a common language be developed that recognises the sensitivities of adolescents and yet also presents a solid tradition that will support them in their adult years? There can be no single strategy that supports all the needs in school or college. However the chaplain, in leading prayer and worship, needs to establish some common denominators between a fuzzy new age style of spirituality and some of the more explicit claims of Christian belief which many adolescents and adult staff are far from sure about. As well as this spectrum of views, there will be a large number of people who will describe themselves as *agnostic*, if not atheist in their thinking, some of whom will be staff. Further enriching this variety in the school community will be those of other faiths who bring conviction, practices and the beliefs of other traditions to the experience of worship. Balanced against these personal and needs-led approaches to worship is the need to proclaim the Gospel, in season and out of season, with conviction and clarity in a Christian community.

From this broad spectrum of colours the chaplain, like an artist, is called to paint a picture of the presence of God which will awaken a response in each person. Each liturgy and prayer experience will create images that can invite individuals and groups into a relationship with God. Each liturgical experience should move individuals and groups towards a personal encounter with Jesus and the wisdom of the Gospel. Each prayer time needs to create elements that address the differing levels of religious awareness within the group. A basic principle of all worship is that it should begin from life experience and return to it. Therefore any liturgy should begin its planning with an exploration of the experience of the group who will share the liturgy, knowing that somewhere in that experience is the presence of a God in whom we all *live and move and have our being.*[36]

The common denominator in all worship is therefore the experience of the group, reflected upon and searched for the signs of the presence of God. That sense of presence can be expressed in a variety of ways, with a range of images and at many levels of certainty and doubt. As Christians, we believe in a God who came to share life and promised, in the words of Jesus, *to be with us until the end of time.*[37] Therefore God is encountered first of all inside life. That sacred and perhaps devalued presence is revealed most clearly in the experience of hearing the Gospel in life experience and in the sharing of the sacraments within a Christian community. Worship is a loop that takes each person from their own life into mystery and questions and then back, enriched, into everyday life. Worship should return people back to their own life, changed by the energy that comes from touching the depth and meaning of personal experience. The changes that worship can evoke are part of a vocational call to go out and bear fruit and make a difference to others. It is not a therapeutic activity so much as a call to action from within the God-given depths of each young person.

---

[36] Acts 17:28
[37] Matthew's Gospel 28.20

Daily Prayer

The chaplain is not the only one who prays within a school community but he is the one who coordinates the elements of prayer in school life. Prayers at staff briefings are properly led by the headteacher who is the spiritual leader of the school. The normal person to pray with groups in the classroom is the form tutor. The chaplain's role is to resource prayer and its leadership in the school through good material, training and also by modelling good practice. The chaplain will normally have a preferred style of praying but also needs to use a range of prayer experiences, so that the needs of all members of the school community can be addressed.

The chaplain generally provides a regular pattern of prayer for use in the school. This may include daily prayers or a general resource. In schools where technology is well developed the resources may also be available online directly into each classroom. All these resources can seem central to the experience of prayer but they are not the core. The central experience of communal prayer is the genuine sharing of hopes and fears before the mystery of God. Therefore resources only take a group to the threshold of prayer. In the end, it is the confidence, honesty and faith of the group that creates prayer. The real power point in prayer is the personal experience of mystery recognised, valued and shared. One key task of the chaplain, achieved perhaps through resourcing, is to build confidence in those who lead prayer that such an inner-power point exists in every young person. Helping staff and pupils recognise the spiritual relationship that prayer offers can help to build confidence in the simple and profoundly human process of reaching out in faith to touch the mystery and meaning of experience.

Classroom prayer needs to be routine, active, short and integrated into life, if it is to be an effective experience for young people. There are some specific resources available on the Salesian chaplaincy website to support this area of school life.[38]

Large group liturgies

The chaplain's role, as the co-ordinator of main school liturgies, is the provision of direct support to pupils and staff in the creation of liturgies that connect the lived experience of young people with the Gospel and with the sacraments of the Church. As mentioned in the introduction to this book, the chaplain has to protect the sacred nature of these symbols and celebrations. Young people's

---

[38] For prayer resources see www.salesian.org.uk/chap

experience is also sacred and it too needs to be recognised with reverence in the liturgy. The Gospels are sacred and they need to be proclaimed with dignity. The sacramental actions and symbols of liturgy need to be given reverence and due prominence in every liturgy. Good liturgy balances these aspects of worship by appropriate reflection, participation and especially by framed silences.

The starting point for liturgy is therefore listening so that the echoes of the Gospel can be heard in the community and given space in the celebration. Some information on the occasion for the celebration can be provided by the chaplaincy. Perhaps it is a feast of the Church with its own theme or a school event such as the start or end of the academic year. In both cases the chaplain needs to help join the school experience to the wider Church community. Having established a theme that is rooted both in Gospel faith and the experience of young people the chaplain can then help the group of staff and pupils preparing the liturgy. That will involve identifying a Gospel message, creating symbols, telling stories and expressing hopes that lead to prayer. Having generated ideas, a key symbol and Gospel text, the group can then devise ways to express a simple truth through drama, artwork, song, silence and movement. Extending participation through a wide variety of media can allow wider participation from departments and individuals in school.

The whole-school liturgy, or year-group liturgy, should fit into the normal time slots of a school day and generally not extend beyond 40 minutes. This allows the liturgy to be integrated into the school day and be a welcome part of the experience of school rather than be seen as a *disruption* to regular patterns. Readings should be brief, symbols large and self-explanatory and there should be space for two or three framed silences in each celebration. The leadership staff, attending these celebrations, should ensure that behaviour is appropriate. It is not the task of the chaplain to manage behaviour in this context. At the end of the celebration those who dismiss the pupils should avoid as far as possible the reprimanding of groups or giving notices so that the final part of the liturgy, as being sent out to others, is not lost.

There is much more that needs to be said about this area of chaplaincy work. More information can be found on the Salesian chaplaincy website mentioned earlier in this chapter, including planning grids and sample services for busy teachers.

Multicultural working

The chaplain is a key member of staff in supporting the provision of a broad-based community approach to education. The statement below from *Renewing the Vision* for youth ministry applies equally to chaplains in their work within school:

> All ministries with adolescents needs to incorporate ethnic traditions, values and rituals into ministerial programming. Ministry with adolescents needs to counteract prejudice, racism and discrimination by example, with young people themselves becoming models of fairness and non-discrimination.[39]

It is part of the role of the chaplaincy to engage with and celebrate the diversity within the school community. Respecting the traditions of other faiths begins by being aware of their richness and the spiritual rhythms of their year. Finding time to appreciate these is one way of modelling the kind of understanding that is needed in a post-colonial world and a way of witnessing to the Gospel by welcoming the stranger.

In a similar way, the *Department for Children Schools and Families* made the following statement about faith schools and inclusiveness.

> We confirm our commitment to continue to work together, with schools with and without a religious character to improve the life chances of children, to build bridges to greater mutual trust and understanding and to contribute to a just and cohesive society, while nurturing children in their faith and as engaged citizens.[40]

Since the *Education and Inspections Act 2006*[41] every school is expected to create community cohesion. The broader reach of schools into the local community, in the years ahead, is likely to create more opportunities to engage with the local community and the chaplaincy is well-placed to help a school increase its cohesiveness. The natural partners of the chaplaincy in the local community will always be the parishes and the primary schools they support. This is the first point of contact in the local community. The clustering of schools, around key issues and training needs, provides further options for building

---

[39] Renewing the Vision: A Framework for Catholic Youth Ministry. Washington 1997. p 23.
[40] Faith in The System DCSF Publications 2007
[41] http://www.dcsf.gov.uk/publications/educationandinspectionsact/index.shtml

cohesion. Beyond those structured links are wide areas for partnership through diocesan, ecumenical and interfaith networks. Chaplains can be a significant part of the whole-school cohesion policy because they have the flexibility to visit and engage with other partners in the local community. In addition the chaplaincy can provide flexible access points for engaging with small groups from the local community.

There is an unfounded sense in some Church schools that being faithful to one's own faith involves rejecting all others. That approach would be an open invitation to sectarian attitudes and prejudice. The life of faith, expressed in all the major religious traditions, offers wisdom and cultural expressions of belief that have enormous value. Whilst we, as Christians, recognise the unique beauty of our own faith tradition it is possible to appreciate and celebrate this diversity without slipping into the erroneous belief that all religions are basically the same. The Learning and Skills Council offers a great deal of help for chaplains, in the area of multi-faith working. The appropriate document can be downloaded from the internet.[42]

Therefore a chaplain should be comfortable with the elements of Christianity that emerge in Judaism, Islam, Buddhism and Hinduism. By recognising the similarities, the bonds of understanding grow and confidence develops to explore differences with respect and appreciation. In this way, the chaplain helps to build a community that is warm and inclusive where each person's unique contribution is affirmed and celebrated.

The last two chapters have proposed a template of skills and attitudes with which a chaplain can develop an authentic ministry in school. The resources of youth ministry, adapted to the more formal setting of the school community, remain at the heart of chaplaincy work. These skills and attitudes provide a framework within which the more personal style of each chaplain can be mapped and understood by those who manage their work. The next chapter will explore how the work of the chaplain might be planned and evaluated in a consistent pattern through the school year.

---

[42] Multi faith chaplaincy Learning and Skills Council November 2007
http//readingroom.lsc.gov.uk/lsc/National/nat-multi-faith-chaplaincy.pdf

Chapter Seven
Planning & Evaluation

The previous chapter outlines many aspects of chaplaincy work that are flexible and non-formal but that does not mean that chaplaincy should not be planned or evaluated. Planning and evaluation can be an expression of a discerning faith and a creative partnership with the spirit in meeting the needs of the school. Therefore school chaplaincy cannot be planned in a vacuum. In fact, a chaplaincy plan and its evaluation needs to clarify where chaplaincy stands in relationship to the whole school, how it reflects specific aspects of a school mission statement and how it hopes to respond to the needs of the wider community, in and around the school.

Planning

Planning, in a Christian community, is a form of discernment that draws the school into a pastoral cycle.[43] The atmosphere of planning is not as much target-led as it is spirit-driven, in responding to the call of God, through careful listening and Gospel-based service of the school community. The observations and suggestions below represent some of the main elements of chaplaincy planning as they might be drawn together into an overall plan. It is just one way of doing planning in chaplaincy. There are many other ways and models available, many of which emerge from the hospital chaplaincy context.[44] Chaplains, leadership teams and supervisors of chaplains need to construct a planning process that fits their own setting and the timetables and traditions that are specific to their school community. The planning approach should always include the following elements in the process, at some stage:

- Listening.

- Establishing priorities.

- Identifying ongoing core activities.

- Targeting specific needs.

- Timetabling for presence and flexibility.

Listening
A school is an amalgamation of many complex individual needs, many interest groups, traditions and even politics. Listening to a complex wall of sound and sometimes silence, can be baffling for those who plan chaplaincy provision. It is

---

[43] See Christian Leadership David O'Malley SDB Don Bosco Publications 2007 page 62
[44] A review of some theoretical models of healthcare chaplaincy. South Yorkshire NHS 2005

easy to hear the loudest voices and even easier to ignore those who may have no voice in the school community. The Christian tradition, on the other hand, sets great store by the marginal voices in a community and expects to hear the Spirit speaking most eloquently through them. Balanced listening needs to pick up voices that are both strong and weak in the school community and it will take time. The chaplain has a role which involves constant listening to groups, to individuals and also to the changing patterns of communication in school. This general listening can lead to impressions that need to be confirmed with others and not just subjective judgements, on the part of the chaplain. For example, a chaplain may want to mention to a teaching colleague that the noise levels in certain classes seem to be increasing, as the term goes on. Others need to corroborate personal impressions, if they are to have the strength needed to inform a chaplaincy plan.

The key question around the process of listening is quite simple. Who does a chaplain listen to? A chaplain will have a natural affinity with certain adults and pupils in the school community, through whom they will absorb much of their day-to-day impressions of the school. That kind of informal listening needs to be enhanced in planning by a more formalised listening, allowing a wider range of people to contribute, in order to engage directly with the whole-school community. A more structured listening approach might involve the chaplain, under the direction of the headteacher and the line-manager, to create listening opportunities in the following key areas:

Table 1 Listening	
Group	Things to listen for and people to listen to
Pupils and staff and their perceived needs	The perceived hopes and fears of pupils and adults in the school community are the starting points for chaplaincy. Listen for hopes, fears, disappointment, anger, frustration, joys and sadness. This can be achieved in structured conversations or through carefully constructed school-wide surveys.
School leadership and planning teams	Recall the mission statement of the school. Identify leadership plans and the spiritual potential of their content and timing. Listen for specific worries and hopes from the leadership and any opportunities they identify to integrate chaplaincy provision into their development planning.

	Regular conversation and a more formal meeting with leadership and governors can help to establish this listening aspect of planning with the whole school.
The needs of the local community	The chaplain works in the school but also beyond it. Therefore listening needs to extend - to parents (perhaps through the PTA) to parish priests and diocese (perhaps in a deanery meeting) to local authority information, to ecumenical networks to agencies such as CAFOD and Fair Trade.
Any unique future opportunities	Listening for planning purposes will also include becoming aware of the possibilities that lie ahead. Events such as the World Cup, a school anniversary or a significant retirement in school can create opportunities that can be integrated into the planning for a chaplaincy.
The emergence of any scriptural models or Gospel wisdom	All those involved in the planning for chaplaincy should also be encouraged to listen for any echoes of scripture in the stories they hear about school and their own feelings and impressions. This listening for the Gospel in life is a vital integrating factor in all chaplaincy planning.
The chaplain's own impressions and experience	The chaplain needs to spend some time reflecting on their own experience, as well as the impressions of others. Sometimes favourite projects need to be reassessed, expectations need to be raised and, at times, lowered. Personal gifts need to be recognised and perhaps relinquished as part of the planning process.

Establishing priorities

Listening is a never-ending process, which continues to inform planning at every stage. At some point, the listening has to give way to the establishment of clearer priorities, without losing the flexibility to respond to changing needs and inspiration. It is important that this filtering takes place in a group-context. There should be a planning group that may not meet except at around this time to ensure a broad-based planning. The group should include the chaplain, the chaplain's line-manager and the headteacher. Beyond that small group, the head of Religious Education may be invited and perhaps a member of the governing body who has particular concern for school ethos. In some schools, where a governing body has an ethos sub-committee, that group might form a more natural and continuous setting for the broad overview of chaplaincy planning.

The task of the planning group will be to establish clear priorities to work towards, rather than generate a detailed plan. The group's challenge is to respond to the perceived needs outlined in the table and, in a prayerful setting, to let the main priorities emerge from discussion. In general the group should identify four or five main priorities and suggest some favoured strategies that might suit the school and its wider plans. Those favoured strategies should also take into account the gifts and availability of the chaplain and the chaplaincy team. This group can help the chaplain to discriminate between core activities that the school needs and short-term projects that may have had their day.

Having established some priorities, this group can allow the chaplain and the line-manager to develop a more detailed plan. This stage is mentioned in some detail later but it does need to return to this larger group to be challenged, sharpened and connected to the wider planning within the school. Some redrafting may be necessary before an agreed plan emerges.

The core activities and the major priorities that emerge from this group need to have clear links back to the mission statement of the school and to the development plan for the school. There should be a chaplaincy thread running through that development plan so that chaplaincy can be seen to be a core part of the school life, to be accountable in clear ways and to be seen to be adding value to the work of the school community. An integrated chaplaincy plan allows schools to highlight their distinctive Christian ethos and it also creates opportunities to draw other staff into involvement in chaplaincy by simply doing what they may have done before but in a more integrated way.

Identifying core activities

It is clear that chaplaincy has a constant task regarding the seven focal points of chaplaincy identified in chapter two. How those seven focal points are acted out in chaplaincy will vary greatly but each of them should find a representation somewhere in the core tasks of a chaplaincy plan. Having these clear core tasks as a chaplain is essential. The priority of each and the way that each is provided within the school will depend upon the needs of the school and the people available. Only a small proportion of chaplaincy is provided through the person of the chaplain. Most aspects are shared with leadership, volunteers and pastoral groups within the school. These areas can help focus the chaplaincy plan and the work of the chaplain in its coordination:

- Spiritual accompaniment.

- Pastoral Care.

- Evangelisation.

- Catechesis.

- Religious Education.

- Liturgical Celebration.

- Parish and neighbourhood liaison.

Simply *being* a chaplain is not sufficient in the busy and structured atmosphere of most schools. A chaplaincy plan should identify a core of activities that give the chaplain a rhythm of working and a pattern of access to a wide range of the school community. A good core activity is one that would be regular, available to a range of different people and easy to provide in terms of preparation and follow-up. Generally it should have a focus around personal, social or spiritual activity rather than academic disciplines.

The rhythm of such core activities should shape the daily timetable and the weekly timetable of the chaplain. For instance, a chaplain may well want to have presence at assemblies or in classroom prayer each morning. Another chaplain, with different priorities, may wish to be present around the pastoral offices in the first half-hour of school. A chaplaincy plan might encourage a chaplain to be in the staffroom for half an hour each day at the same time to engage with a varying population of staff each day. On a weekly basis, a plan might suggest a chaplain should be in the recreation area three times a week, rather than restricted to the chaplaincy base.

More structured links with the Religious Education department and attendance at pastoral meetings will add further shape to the chaplain's role in school. With some careful planning, a chaplain can find these core activities provide a range of access to pupils and an opportunity to work alongside a number of adult colleagues in school. There is, however, a danger in this organisation of the chaplain's core activities. The greatest gifts a chaplain can bring to a busy school are stillness, presence and flexibility. Overloading a chaplain with too many core activities undermines those gifts for the school. Ideally, the timetable for a chaplain should be loosely-packed and focused around personal and pastoral needs. A chaplain should always be flexible enough to respond, more or less immediately, to personal needs - to show a new arrival around the school, to talk with a pupil in a corridor for example. Being a still point in the whirlwind of a school day means that priorities need to be fewer and deadlines longer but both deadlines and specific priorities do need to be there, to give shape to the role of the chaplain.

For most schools, these core tasks will be captured in the line-management and in the job description which will be similar to that of other roles in school. The difference, for a chaplain, is that these core roles need a more regular review since they can change with emerging needs and as a result of changes in the development plans of the school. Line-management will be dealt with, in detail, later.

Targeting specific needs

Listening to the school community, with the Gospel in mind, can generate a wide range of possible projects that respond to specific needs. Some of these possible projects need to be recognised as whole-school projects beyond the remit of the chaplaincy alone. Other projects can be very short-term and fit well with a flexible chaplaincy plan. In one school, for example, the provision of relaxation classes for year eleven pupils prior to exams was a successful project that responded appropriately to a need and could be met with support from learning mentors.

Young people, at each stage of their time in school, should have the opportunity to be challenged through each of the dimensions listed in the previous chapter. Therefore some elements of spirituality, justice and peace, service and leadership, as well as prayer and worship, among others, should be accessible in each age group in the school. It is often not possible to provide these as on-going provision, through the chaplaincy, but they could be made available as short projects in a way that can raise their importance as aspects of Christian living.

One school consciously set up a small twinning-project, precisely because justice and service was under represented in the school experience of the pupils in a certain age group. Another school has established a regular pilgrimage to Santiago in order to focus on the spirituality dimension of older pupils. Choosing specific projects is therefore an art that involves creating experiences to fill out what it means to be a Christian, for young people. Inserting these projects effectively into the school programme and drawing other staff into supporting such projects is another art that chaplaincy needs to practise in order to access a range of areas of school life. A good chaplain will always begin by identifying what is already happening and recognising how it is contributing to the comprehensive youth ministry approach and be careful not to duplicate it for that age range in a way that competes for the attention of young people. By spreading specific short-term projects across a school year that can link to existing good practice and traditions a chaplaincy establishes its own style of working within the school community. Good links with external agencies can also lead to opportunities for students outside school or college, for example a diocesan youth Lourdes group, or the CAFOD leadership scheme. Here the chaplain's role may be simply the mediator of information, with due encouragement and support.

Timetabling for presence and flexibility

Chaplains sometimes complain that most of their work has to be squeezed into too few lunchtime slots. The chaplain who is always busy with small groups at lunchtime is not in the playground, not in the staffroom and not available to enter into conversation with the majority of the school. And yet, lunch time is the only time that much of the chaplain's group work can take place. Being available, free to roam and ready *to waste time* with people is especially useful at break times in the school day. This role is part of the core activity of a chaplain. Therefore chaplains should not timetable themselves at every break time. The number of projects may need to diminish, the scale of the project may be smaller and its duration shorter. Unlike the teacher in the classroom, a chaplain has a duty to the whole-school community and needs to fit specific tasks into the core attitudes of availability and flexibility, especially in responding to individual needs.

The timetable of a chaplain should therefore be loosely-packed and some elements should be moveable. The ideal situation is that the chaplain is always occupied, but can always be interrupted. That requires that a chaplain be well ahead with any deadlines and not get drawn into a last-minute mentality. Another aspect of flexibility involves always having some task to involve others with. When young people are distressed, isolated or unwell having a stream of small tasks can help increase participation in activities, through the presence of pupils who need to take time out. Having flexible tasks ready takes planning, creates community and extends the influence of the chaplaincy. One school chaplaincy built a card-making project out of such occasional visitors to the chaplaincy who did not want to talk but needed activity out of the classroom.

One of the chaplain's skills, in managing work in the school, is to know when to end a project. There are many projects in school that have lost their life and are endured rather than enjoyed. A chaplain needs to remember that most informal groups will have a *sell by date*, they have become stale and need to end at a convenient moment with a good evaluation and celebration. Letting groups go is important for a chaplain if they are to avoid building cliques that only generate resentment in excluded pupils and staff. A group that runs on for a long time will be increasingly likely to be meeting the chaplain's needs rather than the needs of the group or the school. Line-managers of chaplains need to be ready to challenge chaplains in this area and clarify the spiritual and emotional health of such groups.

The beginning and ending of school years and terms are typically very busy for school chaplaincy. Planning large liturgies, welcoming new members to the school community and saying goodbye to others all takes time. When teachers are running down to the last day of term, the chaplain is usually gearing up for liturgy practices, music, drama and other events to celebrate the end of term. These periods of time need further flexibility and some support from the line-manager, in easing any issues.

In making a plan for the chaplaincy year it is advisable to start some projects a week or so later where possible so that the year or the term does not begin with a log jam of unfulfilled hopes. Similarly, there should be space in the chaplain's year for some retreat time and each week should see some designated time for reflection, reading and prayer. The chaplain who is not praying, reflecting and reading is not doing their job in the school. This element of their role needs to be reflected in their timetable on a weekly, termly and an annual basis.

Table 2 Outline Grid for planning a Chaplain's Timetable				
	Activity	Target Group	Frequency	Location
Core activities				
		Target group	Time of year	
Specific projects				

Core activities should cover the seven focal points for chaplaincy outlined in chapter two. Remember that one good activity can achieve a number of different outcomes that could cover a number of focal points. Specific projects should pick up any gaps in the core activities and make the most of any opportunities that emerge in the school year. The aim of this grid is to create a balanced plan that achieves a wide impact in the school and maintains a good weekly rhythm for the chaplain that ensures flexibility and time for reflection.

Evaluation tools for chaplaincy

Evaluation is not simply a functional activity aimed at measuring the costs and benefits of a chaplaincy. It is also a reflective process that opens up new possibilities, uncovers deeper concerns and points to underlying issues that may have lain hidden beneath older patterns of working. In a Christian context evaluation becomes a form of discernment in which God's will is revealed in specific experiences and in patterns of need that come into sharper focus when placed alongside the Gospel in a prayerful atmosphere. Therefore all evaluation in school should have a spiritual and reflective dimension. Chaplaincy is no exception. A range of options are offered below to help a school to assess and build effective chaplaincy. Each has strengths and weaknesses and leaders in school may want to use a number of different approaches to capture the spirit of their own chaplaincy provision.

1 Self Evaluation Format (SEF)
The most familiar format for schools is the one provided through the Catholic Education Service, under its section forty-eight inspection schedule. This format has been adapted to focus on chaplaincy and can be found in the appendices of this book. The advantage of this form of inspection is that it provides the kind of language and accountability that teaching colleagues will recognise. It also gains rapid recognition in the planning structures of the school which will tend to raise the profile of the chaplaincy as a legitimate departmental structure within the school. The evaluation grid also highlights some of the specific concerns and the methods of chaplaincy and enshrines them in a familiar format available to governors and leadership in school. A further benefit of the section forty-eight structure is the possibility of noting developments and the extension of work from year to year in a clear way. For Sixth Form Colleges the Self Assessment Report would fulfil a similar function and can also be modified to allow departments to reflect on their contribution to the spiritual and moral dimensions of the curriculum.

The disadvantage of this form of evaluation is that it can miss the less tangible aspects of chaplaincy work that cannot be recorded effectively in words. Most chaplaincy is relational in nature and the quality of the contact a chaplain creates with individuals and groups needs to be recognised in other forms of evaluation that stand alongside the more formal instrument. For that reason, two contrasting styles of evaluation are proposed, one of which focuses on the process of chaplaincy provision and a third that examines the shape of the provision based on the components of youth ministry.

2 Evaluating the processes at work in a school chaplaincy

This approach relies upon the model of chaplaincy outlined in the introduction and offers a five point criteria for evaluating the process of chaplaincy provision. It can be used to examine the whole chaplaincy provision, a specific area of chaplaincy provision (such as liturgy or justice and peace) or it could be used to examine a specific project. The evaluation questions are laid out in the form of a table, but they need to be explored in a structured conversation rather than as a paper exercise. The evaluation will tease out hidden assumptions and examine the effectiveness of the relational aspect of the chaplain's work. Even though relationships can be difficult to examine in chaplaincy the supervisor should ask for evidence and illustrative experiences where possible in exploring the chaplain's work.

The structure outlined can be used to gain a quick overview of chaplaincy for the whole school and to monitor future developments. It can also be used in a more focused way to explore a specific area of work as a pastoral reflection. Both sets of questions are laid out side by side.

Table 3 Evaluating the Process of Chaplaincy	
Overall evaluation	**Specific Project**
1 Listening to real and perceived needs	
To what extent has the chaplain time for conversation with individuals and groups in school?	In whose perceived needs is this project based?
To whom is the chaplain listening in making judgements and plans?	How far have those needs been checked with a wider group?
Is the chaplain accessible to a wide range of people for informal conversation?	How far is the chaplain listening and planning with others?
What general needs are being expressed by the majority of the school community?	How are those affected by the project given a voice in an evaluation at its conclusion?
2 Guarding individual dignity	
To what extent is the chaplain available for individual needs?	What are the objective principles for the selection of individuals for this project?
What provision is the chaplaincy making for vulnerable members of the school community?	Are vulnerable members of the school community encouraged to engage with this project?
How does the chaplain recognise and celebrate success?	In what ways will the activity of this group be accredited?
How are confidentiality and child protection standards maintained in the work of the chaplaincy?	Does this group's activity fit the normal pattern or need a specific risk assessment?
How accessible and confidential is the chaplain in meeting personal staff needs?	How have individual needs been communicated to other staff in the school?

Evaluating the Process of Chaplaincy	
Overall evaluation	Specific Project
3 Actively and visibly serving the community	
How well does the chaplaincy promote and publicise its work around the school?	Whose real and pressing needs lie at the heart of this project?
What percentage of the chaplaincy work is devoted to justice and service projects?	How widely has its work been advertised in school?
What specific service activities have been used to animate the whole school?	Is there a variety of the school community involved?
What is the general impact of chaplaincy as a witness to Gospel values in school?	Have groups with a similar focus been identified and contacted?
Have opportunities been taken to engage with the local community around identified needs?	How is this project going to lead to long-term provision and change in the school and community?
4 Safeguarding spiritual values	
What are the spiritual values of the school?	How are the aims of this group expressed in spiritual terms?
How does the chaplaincy sustain those values in its normal pattern of activity?	How does the work of this project model aspects of the Gospel?
What visible symbols witness to the spiritual values of the school?	How is individual spiritual maturity developed in this project?
To what extent does the chaplain promote the spiritual values of the school in pupil behaviour, staffing, mission statements and policy development?	How is the work of this project presented to the school as a spiritual activity?
Is the whole-school liturgy provided by chaplaincy celebrated properly and well?	How has the work of this group been linked to liturgy and ritual?

Overall evaluation	Specific Project
5 Rooted in prayer and reflection	
How much time does the chaplain devote to reflection and personal prayer for the school?	To what extent has reflection on the aims of the group happened?
What provision is made across the school to resource personal and collective prayer?	How has prayer been integrated into the general pattern of activity in this project?
How does the chaplain encourage and resource the ability of adults to reflect on their experience in school?	Have specific issues in the group been linked to reflection and prayer? Example - being reconciled, giving thanks.
Has the chaplain been given access to regular line-management and non-managerial supervision?	Have individual issues been highlighted and given time for reflection?

This form of evaluation will be best explored in a conversation between the chaplain and their line-manager at an evaluation point in the school year. The focus of the conversation will be around who the chaplain is listening to. Whose needs are they meeting and what quality of honesty and confidentiality is at work in these relationships. A chaplain will undoubtedly have a number of strong qualities and will be drawn to action in some areas of their role rather than others. The ability of the chaplain to listen, build teams, involve a wide range of people and draw them into spiritual reflection are crucial aspects of this evaluation. Some chaplains will be so busy that they have no time to reflect, to listen to God. Others will be so caught up in listening that they never get into effective action based on what they have heard. The chaplain will also have a tendency to focus on a specific age range. How the chaplain relates across the age range from staff to year seven pupils may throw up some areas of personal development for the chaplain. The ability of the chaplain to recruit others to fill the inevitable gaps in their own giftedness is a further invitation to explore the collaborative element of work in a chaplaincy.

3 Evaluating the shape of chaplaincy

The final approach to evaluating chaplaincy rests on the content of chapter five and six of this handbook. The elements of a relational youth ministry cover a range of different activities that can reveal the overall shape of chaplaincy provision. In general a large school chaplaincy should be able to cover all the aspects of this comprehensive model of youth ministry and apply it also to working with staff. The specific needs of the school may dictate that some aspects have a higher priority than others and the gifts of the chaplain may tend to enhance some areas more than others. The evaluation grid, in table 4, allows the chaplain to assess the work of the chaplaincy plan against the components of youth ministry and identify where the strengths and weaknesses lie in present provision.

The sample in the grid outlines some of the strengths and weaknesses of the author's own chaplaincy work. Each chaplain would need to list all their main activities in the left hand column and then spend some time reflecting on how those activities engage with different aspects of ministry.

Table 4 Evaluating the shape of Chaplaincy									
What aspects of youth ministry are present in the chaplaincy activities listed below?	Community building	Evangelisation	Justice and service	Leader development	Pastoral Care	Prayer and Worship	Multi- Cultural working	Catechesis	Advocacy
Liturgy group	✓	✓		✓		✓			
Fair Trade			✓	✓			✓		✓
Lunchtime drop in	✓		✓		✓				✓
Staff meditation	✓	✓			✓	✓			
Sacramental Preparation	✓	✓			✓	✓		✓	
Assembly support	✓	✓				✓			
Bereavement Support	✓				✓	✓			
Retreat provision	✓	✓				✓		✓	
Totals	7	5	2	2	4	6	1	2	2

Using this grid as a basis for reflection allows practical ways of working to be examined to make them more comprehensive in their impact. The totals in different columns are only a stimulus to reflection and not hard figures. A school in a multicultural area might want to look at a low score in that area and ask if they are missing opportunities to engage with that need. A school with a deprived catchment area would expect to have a chaplaincy with a strong pastoral care element. On the other hand a school with a settled and gifted intake would be expecting to demonstrate a lot of leadership development. The conversation emerging from this kind of assessment might have as much to do with the range of perception of the chaplain as with what is actually taking place. Some chaplains will realise that they can achieve a number of different aims through one activity, others will not recognise that as clearly. The line-manager has an opportunity in this evaluation to help the chaplain to appreciate the range of opportunities in even the simplest activity. This evaluation looks like an exercise in ticking boxes but the conversation that follows that exercise creates an opportunity to reflect on the multiple levels on which chaplaincy work can happen in one single activity or project. Thinking through the complexity of the role and its outcome allows the line-manager to appreciate and celebrate the work of the chaplain. Recognising the undeveloped aspects of the chaplaincy can clarify the specific shape of the chaplaincy and perhaps some development needs for the chaplain in the year ahead.

Focus Groups

Focus groups are guided meetings of varying groups of young people and adults in a school community within which their own needs and experience can be expressed. They are a helpful part of evaluation and planning because they broaden the viewpoint of the chaplaincy and its planning. Short gatherings of small and varied groups with a specific issue-based agenda can help to uncover deeper issues, the impact of the chaplaincy in school or of a specific campaign or service that chaplaincy provides. These small groups of between five and ten people can also help to test a need that is perceived by the chaplain. For example, the chaplain may feel that there is a need for more adult presence in the yard or a different type of assembly structure. Reviewing the reactions of various small groups from different ages in the school might reveal that the issue only lies in year ten or only at a certain time of the school year.

Focus groups can provide some useful planning information fairly quickly. The groups can be gathered adhoc for twenty minutes to gather reactions, ideas and reflections. Such groups not only support planning, they also build cohesion and extend the voice of the students into the shaping of the school. This type of group supports the Christian conviction that it is within the whole community that we discern the spirit and find a way forward. Focus groups provide a planning tool that brings an element of active democracy into the decision making in the school. Further information on focus groups can be accessed at the University of Surrey website.[45]

---

[45] http://sru.soc.surrey.ac.uk/SRU19.html

Chapter Eight
Line Management
&
Non-Managerial Supervision

Line-management models in school are generally focused on the setting and achievement of targets. The sessions happen once or twice a year and lead to a paper exercise in which the appraiser is both an assessor and a developer. This approach has attracted some criticism[46] and is not appropriate in the line-management of chaplains in school for the following reasons:

- The chaplain's task is not easily reduced to identifiable targets in the same way as some aspects of teaching.

- A teacher's line-manager is generally a head of department who is aware of the day to day work in which they are engaged. This will rarely be the case for a chaplain working in a different method and in different places around the school.

- The predictable and timetabled tasks of a teacher allow for an occasional appraisal session to be effective within the general patterns of departmental meetings and classroom observation. The chaplain's work is less predictable, often reactive to specific issues and, therefore, in need of a more frequent and flexible form of line-management.

- Staff development procedures within the school need to recognise the unique needs of a chaplain in terms of supervision and guidance. The chaplain is often the only person engaged in working in a particular way within the school and that can make for a loneliness that has been reported by many chaplains in their diocesan network meetings over many years. What follows is a proposal for an alternative structure of line-management and non-managerial supervision which schools may wish to adopt or to adapt to their specific chaplaincy needs.

The Chaplain's line-manager

The line-manager for a chaplain needs to have a wider range of knowledge and skills than the average teacher in school. The list below outlines some of the preferred qualities:

- A good knowledge of the ethos and policies of the school and its links into Christian expressions of faith.

- A deep involvement with managing whole-school issues and involvement with planning and development in school.

---

[46] See Human Resource Management D Torkington 7th edition. Prentice Hall 2008

- An awareness of the methods of chaplaincy, informal education and the use of group work and volunteer development.

- Developed skills in listening, affirming, giving feedback and challenging.

- Awareness of the support networks for chaplaincy at diocesan and national level as well as a broad awareness of training opportunities in spiritual and pastoral disciplines.

- Sufficient personal authority in school to gather an honest assessment of the chaplain's impact in school from parents, adults in school and pupils.

The above list suggests that the headteacher may be the most appropriate person to manage a chaplain. However given the need for more regular and detailed sessions another person within the leadership group may be more appropriate in order to maintain a more regular rhythm to the pattern of supervision.

Frequency of meetings

The pattern of supervision meetings will depend to some extent upon the experience of the chaplain and the nature of the work that is involved. Even an experienced chaplain would benefit from a minimum of one session every half-term to review and to plan. A chaplain in the first year of their work would benefit from a regular monthly meeting in which some coaching and information-sharing might also be involved.

The frequency of meetings might also depend upon the nature of the chaplaincy work. Some chaplaincy provision adopts a very regular pattern that ties in closely with the work of some departments and follows a predictable rhythm. Other chaplaincies are more varied and work on a project basis or perhaps become a lead focus for some school-wide campaigns. The more complex or varied the chaplain's work becomes, the greater is the need for supervision.

The frequency of the supervision may not be spread evenly throughout the chaplaincy year: The beginnings and endings of school years are especially busy periods for chaplains. Also, there are times when many pieces of work come to an end or group tasks are handed on to new groups of pupils. These times are especially rich moments for reflection, support, celebration and guidance within the line-management context. In the light of such reflections a rule of thumb might be that a chaplain should have a line-management session at least every six weeks but sometimes more often when work is complex or when an overall plan is being formulated.

A line-management session

In general the line-management session needs to be a business-like exchange with clear aims and objectives. Both the manager and the chaplain need to prepare for the session through gathering their reflections on the experience and impact of the chaplaincy and any hopes or concerns that they might have. Following a fixed agenda will help to give a consistent shape to the meetings that have as a background the general job description of the chaplain as well as an action plan that has already been agreed. If no action plan has been identified that should be the task of the first meeting.

A fixed agenda would usually include the following six points:

- A brief review of work from the chaplain which would include any significant successes, struggles, issues or concerns.

- Overall feedback from the line-manager of the impact of chaplaincy within the school in the last six weeks including an opportunity for praise and recognition of work done and any concerns that might have arisen.

- An update on progress on a chaplaincy action plan. What has worked, what has not? What needs more time and what needs to change and what might need to be dropped from the plan? These short-term priorities are an essential anchor point for the chaplain that helps to maintain focus and boundaries in their work.

- A look ahead in the school diary to the next twelve week period to identify opportunities, issues and areas to be explored before the next meeting.

- Opportunities to flag up any issues around training and skills that will help develop the chaplain's effectiveness in school.

- A formal note made about any changes to the plan and a date for the next meeting.

This meeting is focused around the plan and the performance of the chaplain. It is not a counselling session for the chaplain. Within this context a manager may well have to bring up issues of professional misconduct, inappropriate behaviour, failure to meet deadlines, lack of initiative and it therefore needs to have a professional format and have recorded results which are agreed by both parties. It is also a place where the chaplain's work is formally recognised and recorded in a way that gives it an official profile and an opportunity for affirmation and appreciation. A good line-manager will attempt to focus the work of the chaplain on behalf of the school around a few key issues which will have roots in the development plan of the school. Whilst the chaplain needs space and flexibility to operate informally, the ability to focus on one or two key issues helps the school and connects the chaplain to a whole-school pattern of working.

Two meetings with a specific focus

During the year there is great benefit for the chaplain and the line-manager in changing the focus of this meeting. Having a more intense or focused meeting helps to bring the ideas of chaplain and line-manager into harmony about the role and priorities of chaplaincy beyond the immediate plan. One way to conduct this more reflective exercise is to use one of the evaluation tools in chapter seven of this book. Two other approaches can be useful and are described below.

The pastoral reflection

Sometimes a specific incident or experience raises a complex reaction within the chaplain's work. It could be a dramatic event that disturbed the chaplain or a surprisingly successful event. An event that is surprising or apparently complicated is likely to be a good focus for a pastoral reflection. The line-manager may well recognise such events before the chaplain and may need to invite them to consider their experience under the following headings:

- What happened?

- What did you do and why?

- What were your feelings before, during and afterwards?

- What Gospel stories or themes are raised by this experience?

- What does this experience say about you as a chaplain?

- What would you do the same, and what would you do differently next time?

- Does this experience suggest any changes that need to be made in school?

The opportunity for a chaplain to reflect in depth upon a specific incident can help the line-manager to understand the day to day thought processes of a chaplain and to assess the strength of their professional boundaries in working with people. The discussion arising from this reflection can also create opportunities to affirm the skills of the chaplain and also correct any misconceptions or attitudes they may bring to the work.

A session like this needs preparation from the chaplain and ample warning so that the reflection can be written down by the chaplain before it is shared in the session.

Multi-rating session

This approach demands some preparation from the line-manager but it is time well-spent on behalf of the chaplain. In this meeting the line-manager brings feedback from a wide range of people in the school community about the impact of the chaplain. Much of the time the chaplain works without clear feedback and with groups that form and dissolve with regularity. It is not easy for the chaplain to generate feedback on their own role but it can be very helpful if the line-manager can do this.

This approach is sometimes called 360° feedback because the line-manager is asked to gather impressions from a wide range of those with whom the chaplain works. That might include parents, pupils, teachers, administration staff, catering staff, caretakers, parish priests and diocesan groups. From among this range of individuals the line-manager has a brief confidential conversation about the impact of the chaplain and any concerns people may be having. The line-manager may identify a repeated concern and follow that specifically through a number of people by clarifying what the issue is with different people. In those discussions the line-manager needs to reassure the speaker that their views are confidential and any content will remain anonymous. In contrast to the previous approach, nothing is written down except perhaps some bullet points for the line-manager's own use.

Giving the feedback the line-manager needs to present points that have been repeated a number of times rather than sharp specific points that may identify the person in the discussion from which they arose. The outcome of the meeting may well hold some useful information for the chaplain on what impact they are making in the school. This feedback can also help the chaplain to identify where some small relational changes may pay dividends in effective chaplaincy work. The approach also helps to raise the profile of the chaplaincy across the school as a unique service in the school community and therefore strengthen the ownership of chaplaincy across the school.

Non-Managerial supervision

Non-managerial supervision is a strange term based on a negative. It is an emerging practice, especially among chaplains, to have access to a third party beyond the immediate school community, with whom they can share the experience of working as a chaplain. Therefore it is both a person-centred and a role-centred reflection and shares some of the aspects of line-management.

The list below shows an overview of the main focal points of supervision[47] and the breadth of concerns it may raise:

- To provide a regular space for the supervisees to reflect upon their work.

- To develop understanding and skills within the work.

- To receive information and another perspective concerning one's work.

- To receive both content and process feedback.

- To be recognised and supported both as a person and as a worker.

- To ensure that, as a person and as a worker, one is not left to carry unnecessarily heavy burdens alone.

- To have space to explore and express personal distress, that may be brought up by the work.

- To plan and utilise their personal and professional resources better.

- To be pro-active rather than re-active.

- To ensure quality of work.

One of the most important aspects of this type of supervision is the safety it can offer for honesty and insight not only for the person as an individual but for the chaplain in reporting the impact of their relationships and role in school. The authority for this setting comes from the skills and training of the supervisor who needs to operate within a defined code of ethics that protects both parties in the conversation. A chaplain will inevitably absorb the needs and feelings of many people around the school community, carrying secrets as well as the effects of bereavement and general unhappiness that ebbs and flows in all communities.

---

[47] Hawkins, P. & Shohet, R. (1989) *Supervision in the Helping Professions. An individual, group and organizational approach*, Milton Keynes: Open University Press.

Having a safe place to take such private knowledge is psychologically healthy and essential to an ongoing professional approach to chaplaincy.

The choice of supervisor needs to stay with the chaplain. They will need to feel at home with the person and be able to work honestly and effectively with them. The supervisor also needs to have a background in spirituality and an ability to appreciate and integrate scripture and faith issues into the working experience of the chaplain. The local diocese will have a coordinator of chaplains who will be able to support the search for an appropriate supervisor outside the school. Such a supervisor should also have had some training for the role, or at the very least an extensive experience of chaplaincy and education. A list of diocesan coordinators for the Catholic Church is available at www.acce.org.uk. Anglican chaplains can find general support at www.schoolchaplains.org.uk.

The purpose, style and focus of these sessions need to be negotiated between the supervisor and the chaplain. Generally the school should be assured of the professional status of the supervisor before paying the costs for at least four sessions per year. Bills for each supervision session should be invoiced directly to the chaplain's line-manager for payment.

The benefits of non-managerial supervision

A school has a valuable asset in a chaplain. The role adds a unique presence, flexibility and a set of skills to the school community that links ethos to practice, and school to Church. Sister Barbara Brent describes the role of the chaplain as, at times,

> A very lonely one: therefore there is a need for a variety of support networks where chaplains can meet.[48]

The need for a safe place to manage the feelings and tensions that are absorbed in school will help the chaplain to be more resilient and realistic. The provision of this type of support means that the line-manager can maintain a primary focus on the action-planning and formal role of the chaplain without ignoring the more personal issues that may evolve for the chaplain.

The chaplain's job description is very demanding in so far as it invites the chaplain to model Christ in the school on a daily and public basis. They are asked to walk with people as another Christ, they are asked to live their ideals

---

[48] Sister Barbara Brent RJM *School Chaplaincy - Some Reflections* The Pastoral Review January/February 2005 Tablet Publishing Company

in a public forum. This puts a spiritual pressure on chaplains to rise above their own weaknesses and live vocationally in every relationship in the school. The opportunity to take the personal cost of this role into a safe place where spiritual energy can be refocused will have long-term beneficial effects for the school as well as the chaplain in the sustainability of the role and the chaplain's effectiveness over time.

The Call
to Embrace Failure

(A Personal Postscript)

Much of this book attempts to set out a pattern of good practice which will lead to the establishment of an appropriate and effective chaplaincy. It has been concerned to integrate chaplaincy into a system where measurable outcomes emerge from identifiable targets, making chaplaincy accountable for the resources invested in it by the school. The danger of this managerial approach is that it accepts a superficial definition of success that misses the richness of a Gospel faith based on the failure of the Cross. This reflection is offered as an antidote to the present culture that takes a superficial view of education as concerned only with the visible, measurable and repeatable outcomes of instruction and examinations. This reflection is also offered to chaplains personally as an encouragement to see failure as an educational tool and a vital part of the process of chaplaincy. A chaplain who always achieves the desired outcomes and has not embraced failure in a public forum is a miracle worker who probably is not witnessing to the full breadth of Gospel faith – a chaplain who might be missing an opportunity for solidarity with the lost and lowly members of the school community.

There is a story about a man who wanted to tidy up his lawn after moving into a new house. He treated the lawn for weeds, got rid of the moss, fed the lawn and re-seeded areas that were worn. After a year of hard work he had still failed to get rid of a persistent growth of dandelions that emerged even stronger from every treatment. He read books and took advice from the university who gave him specific instructions. When these instructions failed he wrote back to the university to ask what he should do next. The university replied by return email: **learn to love the dandelions**.

There is much wisdom for chaplains in that story because, in the end, chaplaincy is not about plans or targets but about relationships, it is about learning to love. Recently I have been running a small year-seven prayer group each Wednesday lunch time. It is a lively experience and one that did me as much good as it did the young people. However it failed because, as a chaplain. I was finding it hard to maintain a constant presence. So in the second term it began to falter, no other staff member was available to run it. Eventually I had to end an experience that was life-giving for everyone concerned. As a chaplain, I felt awful about letting the young people down and not being able to sustain a commitment. I met with the group and apologised and explained my situation and how upset I was not to be able to provide the promised experience. They in their turn expressed their disappointment but forgave me for letting them down. In the end, the experience of failure helped me to be forgiven by the pupils and the connection with them was sustained. They also learnt to be honest about their feelings and had an experience of choosing to forgive an adult in school. The project was a failure but the learning happened and perhaps it went even deeper than a successful prayer project. Failure can achieve more than success when a broader and more spiritual view of work is embraced. If a chaplain can recognise the value of failure they can also stand by pupils and colleagues who have failed and present that broader view to them at the appropriate time. Of course there may well be a gap between a failure and its fruits and, as educators, we are called to live by the faith that turned the failure of the Cross into the embrace of a loving God. In the story of the Cross the gap between Cross and Resurrection was only three days. The fruits of struggle and failure in school may well emerge many years later in the lives of the young when the educator is not around to witness them. A chaplain lives by faith that all failure is fruitful and nothing is ever wasted by God.

Failure reaches deeper than any failed plans into the depths of a chaplain's own spirit. Chaplains try to work informally and draw learning from all their relationships. The projects and patterns adopted by a chaplain will uncover personal strengths and weaknesses in a chaplain's personality. The fault lines of their own spirit will be projected into their public work in school. For me that means that anxiety will be a constant burden and a drain on energy. I find that in some areas of the chaplaincy role I bring a tension that inhibits the development of the work that needs to be done. My colleagues find that anxiety frustrating and they have to work hard at collaborating with me when I am in that anxious state. For other chaplains there may be different issues: anger, depression, disorganisation, narrowness of spirituality, pride and so on. The chaplain has to recognise that the whole of their personality is at the service of the Gospel including the weakness that makes them more real to others in the school community. People who only live out their ideals and minimise their own mistakes remain two dimensional in their relationships with others. When personal weakness is embraced and admitted, a person can be seen to have a darker side and they take on more depth. Such a person becomes an educator of the heart as well as of the mind. The failures of a chaplain can therefore strengthen their purpose and widen the field of their mission.

I am not suggesting here that chaplains should abandon any professional boundaries, but simply be ready to admit their own failure appropriately in the context of work in school and with pupils. The culture of success in which schools operate at present is, at times, fearful and more likely to crucify the lowly than it is to nurture them into life. A chaplain who can recognise failure can be part of the antidote to that success culture. With inspections, appraisal, and constant measurement there is a tendency to gloss over failure and avoid it. A lot of effort is spent in presentation of progress in school in such a way that failure is eliminated and a distorted picture of reality is projected onto results and evaluations. But, like the dandelions, failure has a way, of persisting. As a chaplain I have to learn to love it. In the Christian faith everything is grist to God's mill, including failure. The Eucharist we celebrate reveals the presence of Christ through the crushing of the grape and the wheat. Christ is revealed through the defectiveness of plans and procedures as much as through their success.

I am glad that chaplaincy has an inbuilt capacity for failure that is greater than that of other roles in the school. This tendency to failure comes about from the informal, personal nature of the task. People approach chaplains because they feel they can get on with them and some people avoid them because they do not feel comfortable with them. Yet the chaplain has to make the first pastoral move towards all the individuals and groups in the school community. The chaplain takes a daily risk of wasting time, offering help and providing experiences that will often be rejected. The rejection is personal because the offer is made in an informal context. The rejection goes deep because it will have happened because the shadow side of the chaplain's personality will have been detected. Therefore a chaplain learns about their own limitations on a daily and a personal basis through the mirror of relationships in school.

The stripping away of any illusions within the chaplain leads to a recognition of the need for teamwork in this role, not just to be effective but also to be healthy. The chaplaincy role is a rollercoaster of a spiritual journey lived out in the formal structure of an academic community. The experimentation, risk-taking and personal investment in chaplaincy will throw a chaplain into many dramatic highs and lows, unknown to those involved in the more predictable patterns of school life. On that personal journey, failure will feel deeper and more significant for the chaplain. That is why a chaplain needs to have clear line-management and regular non-managerial supervision, if they are to remain healthy. Failure is not negative in Christian spirituality. Failure is a road that brings us step-by-step to the rock bottom of our lives and to absolute dependence upon God. On that solid foundation an eternal relationship with God and all humanity can be safely built. Chaplains who embrace failure when it comes along with honesty and courage become teachers of the heart and spiritual guides that offer a richness and meaning that goes beyond the tinsel town success offered by our post-modern celebrity culture.

Just as Jesus was said to have embraced the Cross I believe that a chaplain has to embrace failure.

Resources

I have not listed many books that address chaplaincy in schools directly because they are few in number. The paucity of material on chaplaincy in school indicates that this is still a developing area of interest. I have included some titles from youth ministry and spirituality sources as well as some educational resources that seem relevant.

Books

Association of Chaplains in Catholic Education	A guide to the employment of Lay Chaplains in Schools and Colleges	Catholic Education Service	London	2004
Best Ron (Editor)	Education, Spirituality and the Whole Child	Cassel	London	1996
Borgman Dean	When Kumbaya is not Enough	Hendrickson	Peabody Mass.	1997
Delgato Laurie (Editor)	Catholic Youth Ministry the essential Documents	St Mary's Press	Winona	2005
Gallagher Jim SDB	Soil for the Seed	McCrimmon	Great Wakering	2001
Gallagher Michael P	Clashing Symbols	DLT	London	2003
Hay David and Nye Rebecca	The Spirit of the Child	Jessica Kingsley	London and Philadelphia	2006
Langford Jon	Can We have a Chat: Working Safely with young people one to one	Grove Books Limited	Cambridge	2006

McCarty Robert	*The Vision of Catholic Youth Ministry*	St Mary Press	Winona	2005
McGrail Peter and Sullivan John	*Dancing on the Edge*	Matthew James	Chelmsford	2007
North Karen (et al)	*Revealed*	Redemptorists	Chawton	2008
Robinson Simon	*Ministry among Students*	Canterbury Press	Norwich	2004
Seligman Martin	*Authentic Happiness*	Nicholas Brealey	Maine USA	2004
Sudworth Tim	*Mission Shaped Youth*	Church House	London	2007
Treston Kevin	*Wisdom Schools*	Creation Enterprises	Wiltston Queensland	2001
Ward Pete	*Liquid Church*	Paternoster	Carlisle	2002
Whitehead Evelyn and James	*Christian Life Patterns*	Image Books	New York	1979

Internet resources

The School Chaplain's Conference	A unique, national and ecumenical association to support all Christian school chaplains http://www.schoolchaplains.org.uk/
The Bloxham Project	Works to foster spirituality in schools http://www.bloxhamproject.org.uk/
Association of Chaplains in Catholic Education	A site with extra material, including self evaluation and tables. www.acce.org.uk/
Salesian Chaplaincy	A site resourced by the author to make prayer and assembly ideas available to all www.salesians.org.uk/chap

Other books by David O'Malley
THE CHRISTIAN TEACHER
CHRISTIAN LEADERSHIP IN EDUCATION
ORDINARY WAYS
PRAYERS TO CLOSE THE DAY
PRAYERS TO START THE DAY
TRUST THE ROAD
VIA LUCIS

Books published by Don Bosco Publications

DON'T ORGANISE MY TEARS	A Bailey SDB
SERVING THE YOUNG	J Gallagher SDB
CHLOE & JACK VISIT THE VATICAN	K Pearce
DVD ROSIE GOES TO CHURCH	K Pearce
BOOK ROSIE GOES TO CHURCH	K Pearce
101 SAINTS AND SPECIAL PEOPLE	K Pearce
MEMORY GAME	K Pearce
OUR COLOURFUL CHURCH YEAR	K Pearce
ROSIE AND KATIE GO TO MASS	K Pearce
ST JOHN BOSCO	K Pearce
LOST & FOUND	M Cunningham SDB
A TIME FOR COMPASSION	M Cunningham SDB
WITHIN & WITHOUT	M Cunningham SDB
SEAN DEVEREUX	M Delmer SDB
DON BOSCO'S GOSPEL WAY	M Winstanley SDB
SYMBOLS and SPIRITUALITY	M Winstanley SDB
GOD OF MANY FACES	M Renshaw FMA
MOVING ON	M J Cooke
MAMMA MARGARET	T Bosco SDB
TEACHER, TEACH US TO PRAY	W Acred FMA
THE WITNESSES	W Acred FMA

Books can be bought from **Don Bosco Publications**
www.don-bosco-publications.co.uk
Phone 01204 308811Fax 01204 306868
joyce@salesians.org.uk